HEART *for the* HOUSE

Dave Patterson

Heart For The House
Copyright ©2023 by Dave Patterson
info@tfh.org — tfh.org
ISBN: 978-0-9903775-0-4

All rights reserved. No part of this publication may be reproduced, distributed, or transmitted in any form without the prior written permission from the author.

Scripture Qutotations
The Holy Bible, English Standard Version. ESV® Text Edition: 2016. Copyright © 2001 by Crossway Bibles, a publishing ministry of Good News Publishers.

Amplified Bible (AMP) Copyright © 2015 by The Lockman Foundation, La Habra, CA 90631. All rights reserved.

New King James Version (NKJV) Scripture taken from the New King James Version®. Copyright © 1982 by Thomas Nelson. Used by permission. All rights reserved.

New International Version (NIV) Holy Bible, New International Version®, NIV® Copyright ©1973, 1978, 1984, 2011 by Biblica,Inc.® Used by permission. All rights reserved worldwide.

New Living Translation
(NLT) Holy Bible, New Living Translation, copyright © 1996, 2004, 2015 by Tyndale House Foundation. Used by permission of Tyndale House Publishers, Inc., Carol Stream, Illinois 60188. All rights reserved.

The Message
(MSG) Copyright © 1993, 2002, 2018 by Eugene H. Peterson

TABLE OF CONTENTS

1	Forward
3	Why We Exist
18	Vision: The Church We See
33	Local Church: It's a Big Deal
44	Belong
56	Presence
76	Grow
90	Generosity
102	Excellence
110	Our City
120	Go
131	Enjoy the Journey
141	Supporting the House
160	Membership: The Church I Want to Join

FORWARD

It was early 1997 when eight of us gathered in a living room to worship Jesus and pray about the future. During those formative days the DNA was instilled and the vision embraced for what would become our church, this unnamed group that is now The Father's House. After many years, battles, victories and losses we are still holding to the original vision and passion to build a church for the Glory of God. Our church is far more than meetings, buildings, programs and a crowd of people. It is the culmination of our mission, vision and values as they lead us to build a visible house for God's presence.

When people come to a church, whether they are new to the faith or believers who are searching for a new home, they are stepping into a culture that has been defined by the leaders and established by the committed members. Whether intentional or by default, all churches create a culture. Church Culture is the culmination of the beliefs, behaviors, values, vision, attitudes, and vocabulary of a community of believers.

A healthy church culture is magnetic and an unhealthy church culture is a repellent that can even be toxic for those who stick around too long. Our goal is to create a healthy, Christ exalting culture and to be clear on the kind of church we are building. I believe this is the number one way we can help people to make an informed decision as they prayerfully consider joining our church.

We believe joining, supporting and being released into ministry in the local church is a clear scriptural pattern that requires two things:

1. The leading of the Holy Spirit.
2. The wholehearted commitment of the person joining. Everyone is welcome at our gatherings, but I don't want people to join our church because they are bored or couldn't find a better church. I want people to join with us because the Holy Spirit is leading them, joining them to this body and planting them in the house! As it says in Acts 2:47 (ESV), "And the Lord added to their number day by day those who were being saved."

We are asking God to draw, save, deliver, heal and plant in the house, those who are passionate about our vision and committed to invest in the greatest organization and organism on the planet: the local church!

In the following pages you will find the essence of our mission, vision and values. These are the building blocks of our past and the compass for our future, the things that make our hearts beat faster and the reason we exist. My prayer is that God would speak clearly to you about the value of the local church and give you a life-long passion to get planted in one. If you are searching for a church with big vision and a passion for Jesus, this might just be your house.

Chapter One

WHY WE EXIST

"The Father's House exists so that people far from God can find life in Christ."

We have been called and designed to do far more than exist. We have been invited by Jesus Christ to "have life, and have it to the full" (John 10:10 NIV). "Why we exist" is referring to why we have a church, gather every week, give our time and resources to a cause bigger than all of us and persevere through any and all circumstances. Behind every decision, permeating every investment, and determining every major event and program lays the motivation of our mission.

The term "mission critical" is used to describe something that must take place in order for the system or organization to survive. If the essential element is absent, nothing else works!

If Chick-fil-A runs out of chicken, game over. If FedEx no longer prioritizes timely delivery, the company will cease to exist. If Netflix ceases to release new material, the subscriptions will grind to a halt, and on and on we could go. Then, why is it that many churches can survive for years, even decades, without seeing anyone come to faith in Jesus, be baptized in water, and discipled?

People finding faith in Jesus and growing in their relationship with Him is our "mission critical." If people are not being saved, redeemed, rescued from a life of sin and redirected in their eternal destiny, then our system is broken and nothing else really matters.

MISSION IS THE MAIN THING

Any self-respecting corporation, business, or company that is making a difference, having a global impact, and moving many people and resources in the same direction, has a mission statement. If you are a business owner without a mission statement I would strongly encourage you to take the time and energy to craft one. Without a mission any company can and will eventually get sidetracked, become irrelevant, or be run over by the competition. There must be a central purpose and foundational impetus that keeps things in perspective and determines future behavior. Here are a few mission statements that affect you either directly or indirectly every day.

> "To organize the world's information and make it universally accessible and useful." – **Google**

> "To give people the power to share and make the world more open and connected." – **Facebook**

> "To bring the best personal computing experience to consumers around the world." – **Apple**

"To help people save money so they can live better." – **Walmart**

"To inspire and nurture the human spirit – one person, one cup and one neighborhood at a time." – **Starbucks**

As a church, retail chain or producer of coffee, you should create a mission statement clarifying why you exist based on what is critical to your company or personal life.

I would encourage you to consider your life, your calling, your goals, talents, giftings, and the stewardship of your life that will one day give an account to the Lord. Then, based on all you have been entrusted, craft a mission statement for your life that will be an anchor for your decisions and set the course for a life worth living.

OUR MISSION IS CLEAR

I'm sure you could finish the line, "Your mission, should you choose to accept it..." This means, according to the plot of the movies, that the mission is already resolute and the critical elements that decide whether or not it will be a success have been predetermined. So it is with the gospel message and the mission of the Church. When Jesus gave His departing instructions to His disciples He gave them what we now call the Great Commission, which is the mission critical of every Christ-follower, every disciple and every church!

> Then Jesus came to them and said, "All authority in heaven and on earth has been given to Me. Therefore go and make disciples of all nations, baptizing them in the name of the Father and of the Son and of the Holy Spirit, and teaching them to obey everything I have commanded you. And surely I am with you always, to the very end of the age." **Matthew 28:18-20 (NIV)**

WHAT'S AT STAKE?

There are certain topics from the Bible that are in fact realities, yet they are extremely uncomfortable when we consider the ramifications. We love our friends and families but we don't like to think about what eternity will be like for those who reject the forgiveness of Jesus and live for themselves. We all want to believe that everyone goes to "a better place" when they die but that is not a biblical truth. If eternity with God in a literal heaven or separated from Him in literal hell is in fact scriptural truth and an everlasting reality, then the stakes could not be higher! When I consider the words of John's vision and revelation at the final judgment, I am moved with awe, fear of the Lord and a renewed motivation to be about the mission we have been given.

> *I saw a Great White Throne and the One Enthroned. Nothing could stand before or against the Presence, nothing in Heaven, nothing on earth. And then I saw all the dead, great and small, standing there—before the Throne! And books were opened. Then another book was opened: the Book of Life. The dead were judged by what was written in the books, by the way they had lived. Sea released its dead, Death and Hell turned in their dead. Each man and woman was judged by the way he or she had lived. Then Death and Hell were hurled into the Lake of Fire. This is the second death—the*

Lake of Fire. Anyone whose name was not found inscribed in the Book of Life was hurled into the Lake of Fire.
Revelation 20:11-15 (The Message)

Not a light read by any means, and I am not trying to be a downer here, but in a culture of religious tolerance and man-made theologies, where so many people are living "their truth", it's very healthy and necessary to solidify what you believe about the judgment and eternal state of mankind. Yes, there are mysteries and varying interpretations of this text and others like it, but I have decided, along with centuries of theologians, scholars, and trusted Church leaders to interpret these verses literally. Jesus spoke more about hell than He did heaven. He wanted His audience and all who would follow to **be clear on the mission and clear on the consequences**.

Jesus gave His life for all of humanity, not just a select few. The Bible clearly tells us His intention regarding the eternal state of humanity:

The Lord is not slow in keeping His promise, as some understand slowness. Instead, He is patient with you, not wanting anyone to perish, but everyone to come to repentance.
2 Peter 3:9 (NIV)

If our mission is truly going to be the ongoing motivation for our actions then we must believe that God wants all to hear the gospel message, turn to Jesus and live with Him for eternity.

THE CHURCH IS GOD'S PLAN A TO RESCUE A BROKEN WORLD

Yes, God can and has spoken through nature, circumstances, and even animals!

He has given people dreams of Jesus in the night and sent angels straight from heaven to proclaim salvation. Yet, the primary way God reaches those far from Him is through the Church. This happens when the Church is carrying out the great commission of loving people, preaching the gospel and making disciples.

For "Everyone who calls on the name of the LORD will be saved." But how can they call on Him to save them unless they believe in Him? And how can they believe in Him if they have never heard about Him? **And how can they hear about Him unless someone tells them?**

Romans 10:13-14 (NLT)

For since in the wisdom of God the world through its wisdom did not know Him, God was pleased through the foolishness of what was preached to save those who believe.
1 Corinthians 1:21 (NIV)

THEOLOGY MATTERS

I'm not trying to pick a doctrinal fight or drill down too deeply into this subject in this setting, but allow me to address the topic of sovereignty vs. free will for just a moment. We believe that God is completely sovereign, and within His sovereignty He gave every human the free will to accept or to reject the love, forgiveness, and person of Jesus. If the only people getting saved, according to the teachings of Calvinism, are "pre-destined" to do so with or without our help, then it seems to defeat the effort and urgency of the mission! And yes, I know I'm oversimplifying a complex theological conundrum, but I have a point here. If we are convinced that souls are at stake, that eternal hell is a real place, that the Church has been entrusted with the message of redemption, and that people will either live or die based on our fulfillment of the Great Commission, then we should be highly motivated in our mission!

I fully believe that when **John 3:16** says "God so loved the world that He gave His one and only Son, **that whosoever believes...**" the "whosoever" is the every, any, and all who believe, not just the "whosoever" of the elected or pre-destined for salvation. I hope I'm not confusing you here but I simply believe that when **2 Peter 3:9** says, "God does not want anyone to be destroyed, but **wants everyone to come to repentance**," that everyone means the every, any, and all who will respond to the Gospel. The way we pray, give, preach, live, build the Church and tell others about Jesus has eternal consequences. This theological position is a great motivator in our mission!

MISSION DETERMINES BEHAVIOR

At The Father's House, we invite people every weekend (perhaps not at every service but usually at most of them) to make a decision to come to Jesus, turn from sin and accept the gift of salvation. I've heard all the arguments as to whether or not we should use this method at our services, as "altar calls", as we know them in the modern church, are not a clear pattern in the New Testament Church gatherings. So, people have made comments or asked these questions over the years like:

"Are people truly being saved during those moments?" "Will most of them really stick with it?"

"Isn't this just an emotional response that involves manipulation?"

"Where do you find in the Bible someone praying the 'sinners' prayer'?"

As far as the technique and salvation moment protocols like: eyes open, eyes closed, stand up, stay where you are, lift your hand, come down to the front, say a prayer out loud, believe in your heart and when you are ready, confess Jesus. These are all personal preferences of the one preaching the message and should not be over-scrutinized or attempted to canonize. Whether or not someone is making a true, heartfelt, faith-filled decision that will change the course of their life and eternity is not ours to judge or speculate. Our job is to preach the Gospel and introduce people to the Savior, giving them an opportunity to respond to His love and turn to Jesus. This process not only happens during the weekend services but through small groups, recovery groups, youth ministries, conferences and a variety of gatherings that are happening all the time. Every week, we prioritize the process of training **new believers**, helping them through small group discipleship, and systematic learning environments such as Essentials, Discover, Celebrate Recovery, Biblical Studies Program, and other venues. The mission is not just about the event or salvation experience but the nurturing and training of those trying to figure out this journey of faith. Our job is to preach and invite, the Holy Spirit does the rest. This is what keeps the Church growing, full of life and keeps us on mission!

Throughout the years we have had **Baptism Weekends** where dozens, sometimes upwards of 75 people in one weekend, would be baptized in a public setting, declaring their faith and going public with that decision. Now, at our current location, we are baptizing someone every service, every weekend, as well as special events after summer camps that become mass baptism events. We are grateful for what the Holy Spirit is doing through our church as we stay focused on the main thing and live out this clear New Testament mandate.

> *Each of you must repent of your sins, turn to God, and be baptized in the name of Jesus Christ for the forgiveness of your sins. Then you will receive the gift of the Holy Spirit.* **Acts 2:38 (NLT)**

WHO IS THE CHURCH FOR?

When we begin to ask the question, "*Who is the Church for?*" it becomes clear in Scripture that the Church is not for "church people." It was never God's intention for the Church to be a gathering of people who share the same values, lifestyles, and doctrine for the purpose of becoming a society or club that excludes everyone who does not believe or behave the same way. If we get "on mission" we will no doubt, see many people coming together who are in all stages of brokenness, confusion, and pain.

It's been said of Noah and the ark that "*it was undoubtedly a messy place, but it was the only boat afloat, and so it is with the Church.*" It may get messy and that's okay. It gets awkward at times and there are not always simple answers to complicated issues, but that's all right. **Our objective is not to have clear lines of who is in and who is out, but to create a clear path to Jesus, to build environments where "those far from God can find life in Christ."** We have accepted the mission, and we are committed to keeping the mission clear.

Will you join us? If what I have described in this first chapter is biblically solid and resonates with eternal truth and consequences, then, it means there could not be a more important task and opportunity to invest our lives in them to reach people far from God and build the Church that Christ is returning for, I would unashamedly ask you to go all-in and help us prepare a bride for the King. Give your time, your passion, your finances, your faith, your commitment, and your very existence to co-labor with Jesus in the great commission. Then, at the end of your life or when we stand before the throne of God, you will have truly lived a life well invested with no regrets!

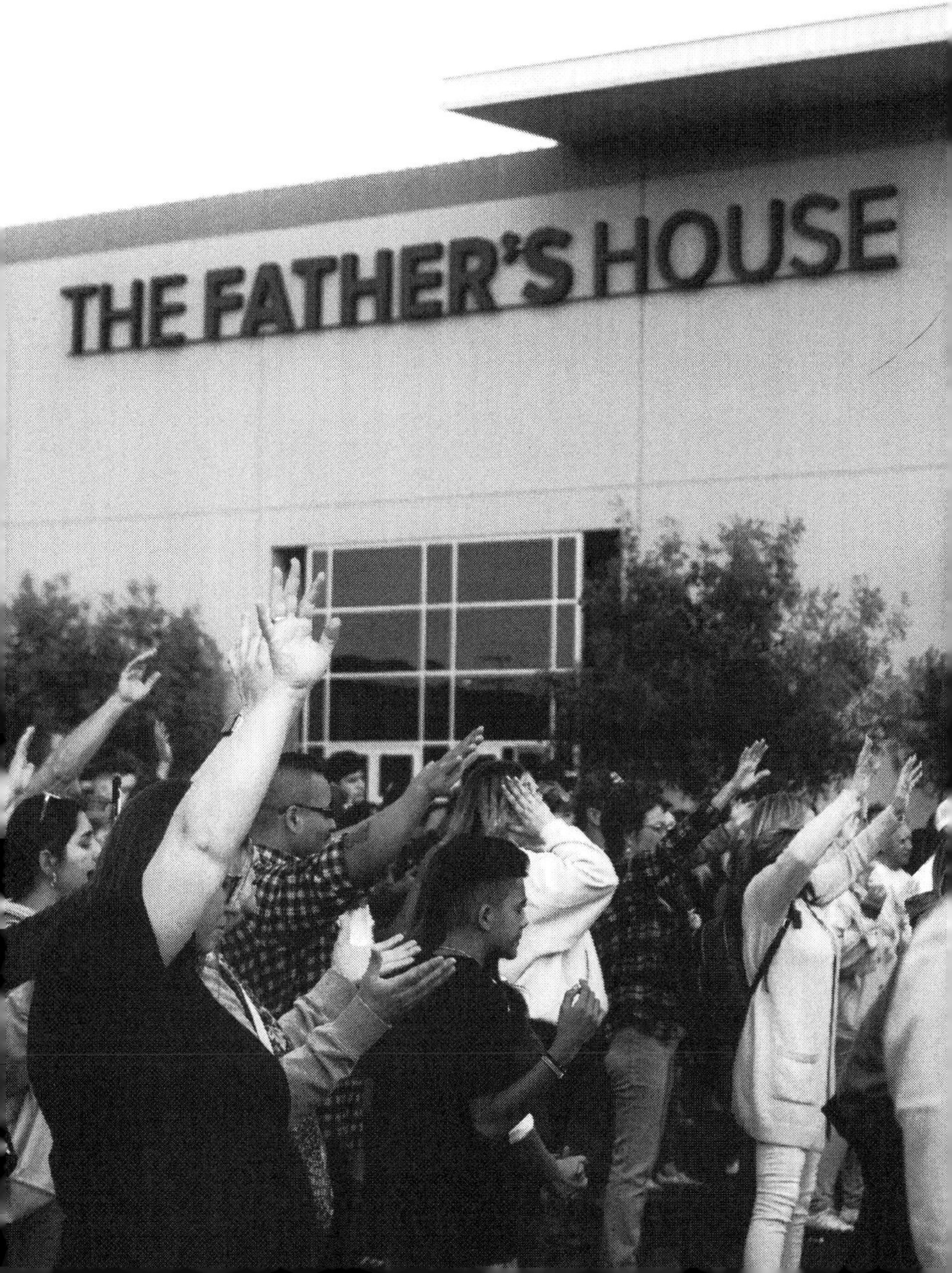
THE FATHER'S HOUSE

VISION: THE CHURCH WE SEE

Chapter Two

"God is big, so we dream big. We will never insult God with small thinking and safe living."

It's all about vision! Big vision! Companies languish, churches decelerate and become irrelevant, leaders fail to lead well, and your life will lack direction and discipline without vision.

Vision: the act or power of anticipating what is coming.

> *"A mental picture of a preferable future. Seeing the invisible and making it visible."* – **George Barna**
>
> *"A God-given glimpse of the future that ignites passion."* – **Bill Hybels**
>
> *"What could be worse than being born without sight? Being born with sight and no vision."* – **Helen Keller**
>
> *"Where dreams and strategy collide to become reality."* – **Unknown**

Inspired vision is looking at life through the lens of God's perspective.

On a cold morning in 1952, 34 year-old Florence Chadwick had set her goal of being the first woman to swim the 26 mile stretch of the Pacific Ocean from Catalina Island to the California coastline. As she began this historical journey, she was flanked by small boats that watched for sharks and were prepared to help her if she became injured or grew tired. Hour after hour Florence swam and kept a good pace, but after about 15 hours, a thick, heavy fog set in. Florence began to doubt her ability and she told her mother, who was in one of the boats, that she didn't think she could make it. Her mother and her trainer continued to offer encouragement. They told her it wasn't much further, but all she could see was fog. They urged her not to quit. She never had...until then.

They pulled her from the water, exhausted and defeated. Florence later discovered that she had stopped swimming less than one mile away from the California shoreline. Florence explained that she quit because there was too much fog and she could no longer see the coastline. She couldn't see her goal. Then she said, "I think I would have made it, if I could have seen the shoreline."

Two months later, Florence got back in the water to attempt her task once more. This time was different. She swam from Catalina Island to the shore of California in a straight path for 26 miles. The same thick fog set in, but Florence made it because as she swam, she kept a mental image of the shoreline in her mind. In 1952 Florence Chadwick became the first woman to swim the Catalina Channel. She also eclipsed the men's record by two hours!

No matter how you define vision one thing is for sure, we will spiritually, creatively and emotionally die without it. It can be argued that a lack of vision will also shorten your physical lifespan as well. King Solomon said it this way, "Where there is no vision, the people perish" **(Proverbs 29:18 KJV)**.

THE VISION OF THE HOUSE

If people can't see what God is doing, they stumble all over themselves. **Proverbs 29:18 (Message)**

Vision is distinct, but not disconnected, from mission. As we discussed in the previous chapter, our mission has already been defined for us. As believers, in a New Testament church, we do not get to pick a mission like we are at a buffet of various missions. We gladly accept the Great Commission as our marching orders and wrestle through the process of how to best live that out in our culture. The mission is not up for a rewrite!

That's where vision is different. Every church has a different vision of how they will fulfill this mission. Now, before I give you the vision statement of our church, let me share a couple of bits of information that have shaped the way we have crafted this statement. Some of the greatest business leaders and consultants of the largest companies have suggested that it must be brief, to the point, and clearly inspire others to be a part of it. On the other hand, there are also great leaders, like Brian Houston of Hillsong Church Australia, who have written multiple paragraphs to describe the God-given vision for their church.

I believe both are necessary and both are valid. So, with that in mind we've boiled our vision statement down to its irreducible core. The vision of The Father's House is to be **a place where people encounter the reality of God.**

When we first started this journey I was in a time of fasting and prayer regarding the kind of church we would build and what God had put in my heart. The following verse became the foundational scripture for our church and the impetus of all we have done for the past 27 years. (at the time of this writing)

> *"My Presence will go with you, and I will give you rest." Then Moses said to Him, "If your Presence does not go with us, do not send us up from here. How will anyone know that You are pleased with me and with Your people unless You go with us? What else will distinguish me and Your people from all the other people on the face of the earth?"* **Exodus 33:14-16 (NIV)**

The vision of our church is t**o be a place where people encounter both the reality and the presence of God.** This happens through preaching, teaching, small groups, giving away food and clothing, generosity, video production, kindness, hospitality, worship times, prophetic moments, and on and on. There are limitless ways for people to encounter the reality of God. Our vision is to create those places, atmospheres and experiences, always measuring if we are on track by evaluating whether or not people are consistently encountering the reality of God, thus being changed into the likeness of Jesus. That's the vision and the win!

THE VISION RANT

Before our church ever started, I was driving north from Concord, California, on Interstate 80 when I saw a vision of what was to come. I can't fully explain what happened, but for about 5 miles, I could see it clearly and feel it deeply. So much so, that I passed my exit and had to circle back once I regained some composure. During this supernatural stretch of the interstate, I experienced and embodied the vision of what our yet-to-be-church plant would someday become.

Here's a glimpse, and an attempt to define the indefinable. I could see thousands of people gathering around the greatness of Jesus, being transformed by his grace and power, and then going out to change their world! I could see people coming from all directions, multitudes longing to experience the presence, power, beauty, and reality of Jesus. I could see musicians, preachers, singers, artists, missionaries, pastors, leaders, and students all working together to create a place, an environment, a church that was irresistible to the spiritually thirsty. The irresistible factor was not the excellence of the facility, staff, marketing, or style (although all those things are important). The irresistible factor was simply the presence of God Himself! The atmosphere, was charged with faith and joy, the magnetism of the beauty of His church was astonishing, and there was a humility and honor that was palpable. It was a place, a space, a "zone of Glory" that you never wanted to leave.

I was captivated at just the thought of being able to be a part of something so grand, so limitless and so eternal. I was able to stay on the freeway during this vision, but just barely and through many tears. That day, I experienced a true glimpse of a future that is worth living and dying for. Now, for a pastor's kid who had seen many years of brutal, unfruitful ministry, this was truly a miraculous moment and a life altering vision. When we founded The Father's House with four couples in the living room of a friend's house, this vision continued to remain in my spirit. As this revelation was released in measured doses to those God was joining to our church, we began to connect strategy to this God-given-picture of our future.

Remember, in order to fulfill a vision, it requires strategy, time, resilience and big faith. The Father's House has been working toward the vision for many years now and by God's grace we are making some serious headway. At the same time, we live in the paradox of thankfulness for what God has done and the Holy frustration of what is yet to be. We long for the fulfillment of the picture that God has painted deep in our hearts! During this process, we will fight the good fight to keep a clear mental picture of God's desire.

THE CHURCH WE ENVISION

I see a church where Jesus is the center. Jesus is preached, worshiped, loved and revealed for who He is.

I see a church that is known for and consistently encounters the reality of God through the presence and power of the Holy Spirit.

I see a church where people are coming to the saving knowledge of Jesus Christ all the time! Salvations, water baptisms and the stories of changed lives are a continual reality.

I see a church that has such an impact on our communities, through serving the broken and poor and expressing the love of Christ in tangible ways that She cannot be ignored.

I see a church that builds strong families, equips parents, restores and strengthens marriages and becomes a safe haven for all who have been through the pain of a broken home.

I see a church where the supernatural happens naturally. Without hype, smoke, and mirrors or superfluous weirdness, we will simply expect the miraculous and experience the supernatural power of God on a consistent basis.

I see a church that has continual involvement and impact globally. Through sending teams, equipping missionaries, partnering with ministries in many nations and being a channel of resources, we will be a hub for all things missions and truly make a global impact!

I see a church that equips leaders and grows with unlimited vision.

I see a church that empowers young people to be leaders in the church today and in the decades to come.

I see a church that is a continual channel of resources and practices radical generosity. We are blessed to be a blessing and all those connected will experience supernatural provision and increase.

I see a church that is a strong river of fresh worship and creativity. Writers, singers, artists, musicians, worship leaders, and all those who have a part to play in the creative arts, will feel right at home and flourish in their gifting.

I see a glorious Church that Christ is returning for! Are we there yet? No, but we are on our way! We have laid a good foundation, and we are building on the values and vision that God has entrusted us with. We will spend the rest of our lives running toward the vision.

THE VISION STATEMENT IS THE FILTER

One of the questions we ask as a leadership team, regarding events, ministries and investments is, "Was it a win?" We want to make sure that we are accomplishing the objective of our vision statement in all we do. So, we ask ourselves questions like, *"Would we do it again?" and "Was it a good investment of our time and resources in light of accomplishing our mission and vision?" Ultimately, "Did it reflect and reinforce our values?"*

If the answer to any of these questions is no, no, and no, then we simply stop, stop and stop. For example, every year we put on a youth/young adult conference. Although we charge a registration fee, by the time we calculate in promotion costs, travel expenses for our guests, honorariums, time invested by our pastors, maintenance teams, graphics, printing, and the list goes on, we always end up investing far more than we bring in.

So why keep doing something that doesn't pay for itself? This seems like a good and logical business question. The answer is, the youth/young adult conference has always fulfilled the primary goals of our mission and vision statements and is well worth the investment. Here they are again:

> **Mission:** The Father's House exists so that people far from God can find life in Christ.
>
> **Vision:** A place where people encounter the reality of God.

We highly value the process of seeing young people saved, discipled and prepared for a life of serving Jesus and His Church. As we consider a conference, an intern program, a recovery ministry, or a cupcake sale, we can ask these questions:

> *"Are people far from God going to have the opportunity to find life in Christ through our efforts?"*
>
> *"Will people encounter the reality of God through this experience?"*

If the answer to both of these questions is yes, then we will continue to invest.

THE FULFILLMENT TAKES TIME, SO BUCKLE UP!

Although we have seen some amazing things in the life of The Father's House, I have yet to see the complete fulfillment of "The Vision." I've seen glimpses of the fulfillment and enough to continue to move forward with great hope for the future, yet I realize the nature of God's vision for our lives may take years, decades, perhaps the rest of our lives. This is why vision requires strategy and resilience. Once we begin to look through the lens of God's perspective for our future, it is our responsibility to build and implement strategies to fulfill this vision. Remember, **a vision without a strategy is simply a hallucination.** Once we have determined a strategy and implemented the plan, then we are going to need big faith and perseverance. **Galatians 6:9** says, *"In the proper time, you will reap if you do not give up."* This is where most people settle for less than a God-inspired vision for their lives; it's the gap between the vision and the fulfillment, the wait between the promise and the answer. Let me encourage you to continue to keep God's vision for your life clear and constantly before you. It will keep you from settling for less and becoming weary during the waiting. Settle in your heart and mind that the vision God gives you is worth a lifetime of devotion.

Be encouraged when the Scriptures tell us:

> *And then God answered: "Write this.*
> *Write what you see.*
> *Write it out in big block letters so that it can be read on the run.*
> *This vision-message is a witness pointing to what's coming.*
> *It aches for the coming—it can hardly wait!*
> *And it doesn't lie.*
> *If it seems slow in coming, wait.*
> *It's on its way. It will come right on time."*
> **Habakkuk 2:2-3 (Message)**

VISION IS EXPONENTIAL, NOT STATIC

All pastors are asked some consistent questions, especially when the church is growing and a diverse group of people are cruising through the doors. People frequently ask me this 'I'm looking for a new church question, "*Pastor, what is the vision of this church?*" I often feel some pressure, as if this is a leadership test and I must get it right for them to stick around. Although, that is a valid question that deserves a concise and compelling answer, I am hesitant to give a "bumper-sticker" reply to such a broad topic. The reason is that the vision God has given our church continues to expand and develop as He adds more gifted and visionary people. **Vision is a clear picture, but it's not a completed picture. It is exponential as more people are added to the equation. This is where you come in.**

If God is adding you to this church, it's highly probable that the vision I have described in this chapter is resonating within your heart. It's also highly probable that the desires and vision you are carrying will fit well and increase the greater vision of the House. When visionary people combine ideas and resources with other like-minded individuals, the sum is always greater than the parts. Unlimited vision is a powerful catalyst to change the world!

I invite you to join us in our quest for the vision of the House! Bring your talent, passion, and heart for God and let's see what God will do through you, me, and an army of visionaries. It's going to be an Ephesians 3:20 ride!

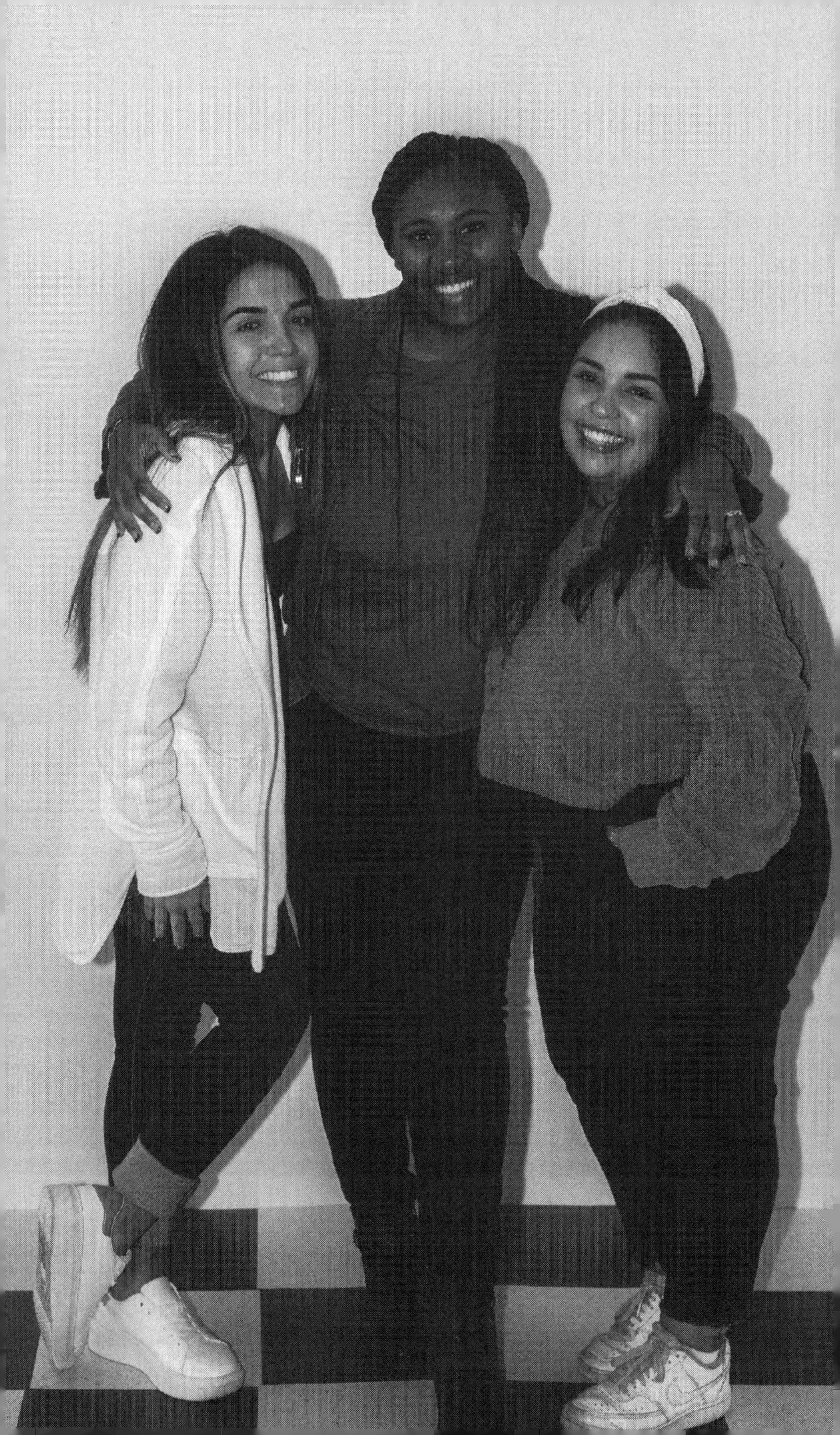

Chapter Three

LOCAL CHURCH IT'S A BIG DEAL

"Christ loved the Church and gave up His life for her." Ephesians 5:25 (NIV)

It has been said, "*The local church is the hope of the world.*" At first read that might appear as a grandiose statement or that someone forgot to mention Jesus. Some would immediately argue that Jesus is the hope of the world and not the Church. The biblical and spiritual reality is that they are inseparable. Jesus and His Church are indivisible in the mission of being the light of the world, the hope of the nations and the means of seeing a lost world come to a loving God.

The Church has been deputized and dispatched to preach the gospel, make disciples, change nations and work side by side with Jesus to build His Church! The Church is His plan, His passion, His vehicle and His design. The church is a big deal to God!

DELEGATED AUTHORITY

I have been given all authority in heaven and on earth. Therefore, go and make disciples of all the nations, baptizing them in the name of the Father and the Son and the Holy Spirit. Teach these new disciples to obey all the commands I have given you. And be sure of this: I am with you always, even to the end of the age.
Matthew 28:18-20 (NLT)

When Jesus commissioned the first group of disciples to *"go into all the world"* **(Mark 16:15)**, He wasn't just speaking to the original team. It was a commissioning until *"the end of the age"* **(Matthew 28:20)**. He told us that we would hold the keys to the Kingdom **(Matthew 16:19)**, have power over the spirits of this age **(Ephesians 1:21)**, the ability to ask anything in His name **(John 14:13)** and delegated authority to get the job done! All of the promises of authority and kingdom advancement are given in context of the Church, the Body, and the Family of God. We experience God's authority in our lives when we are about His business, the business of building His church. The more we connect our passion, our talents and our resources to the central theme of the gospel and the local church, the more of God's authority will be released in our lives.

WHY THE CHURCH SHOULD BE BIG

There are some things I hate. If that seems like an aggressive or offensive statement, let me remind you that there is a list of things, in the Bible, that God hates, so we are on safe ground here. One of the things I hate is when people belittle a big church, putting down what God has brought up, they attempt to deconstruct through deceived thinking, and vicious accusation, what Christ has given His life for and taken first-person ownership of. I love the Church! I love the international and eternal influence of the Church! I love the unstoppable, overcoming, glorious Bride of Christ who is preparing to meet her King. I love when a church has so much growth and influence that it begins to impact its city in unavoidable ways! I love what Jesus is building, so I hate those things that are set on tearing it down. Now, we must be clear that while we do not and should not hate people, we should hate the motivations, lies and destructive conversations that infiltrate the church because of deceived thinking.

The things you hate can be the clearest indicator of what you truly love, and what you hate defines your passion. For example, the Apostle Paul was passionate about the believers and the Church that God had called him to plant and lead, so he was intense in confronting enemies of the work of God.

> *For I am jealous for you with the jealousy of God himself. I promised you as a pure bride to one husband—Christ.*
> **2 Corinthians 11:2 (NLT)**

In light of what Jesus has given for His Church and His claim when He said, *"I will build my Church"* (Matthew 16:18), and in light of the fact that the Church is the hope of the world, not only globally but locally, we should give our lives to build great churches! We should invest our time, resources and our passion to build healthy, Christ-exalting, community-impacting, generous, missions-minded, addict-rescuing, people-restoring, Bible-preaching churches that become the biggest deal in our cities! I believe this with all my heart and oppose the mindset and conversations that attempt to make the church look weak and insignificant.

Now that I've gotten that off my chest, let me tell you some of the reasons why I love big churches.

A BIG CHURCH

Makes an obvious statement about the scope of its mission

Provides more opportunity and has more options (due to finances and resources)

Is social, friendly, and fun (that's my experience & opinion)

Is stable (does not shut down or split as frequently as small churches)

Has exponential creativity and new ideas

Has a large influence in the spirit realm

Experiences greater influence in its city

Is competent at fulfilling the great commission

Financially can do far more globally with world missions
Can launch and sustain effective ministries

Can tangibly make a noticeable difference in the economic condition of its city

Can shape the culture of its region and build a culture with greater diversity

Is outward focused (living beyond survival mode)
Continually models and communicates living life with bigger vision

Now with that list, let me be quick to say that I do not despise small churches! I believe a church should represent a percentage of its community. For example, if you are a pastor in a farming community in the high deserts of eastern Idaho, then a gathering of 30-50 people might be making a significant impact in your community and representing well the name and nature of Jesus in your town. So while there is a place for small churches, there is no valid excuse for a church to stay small when there are thousands of un-churched people within reasonable driving distance. The church size and vision for future growth should represent the community and population where it is planted.

THE CHURCH SHOULD BE UNAVOIDABLE

You are the light of the earth. A city on a hill cannot be hidden. Neither do people light a lamp and put it under a bowl. Instead they put it on its stand, and it gives light to everyone in the house. In the same way, let your light shine before men, that they may see your good deeds and praise your Father in Heaven.
Matthew 5:14-16 (NIV)

Jesus paints the picture of a large, unavoidable gathering of lamps and lights that will not be ignored in a dark world. The Church is a city within a city that cannot be hidden! You should never have to ask 10 people where a good church in town is or where you can find Jesus being exalted. Clearly the Church is to grow in size and impact until ALL CAN SEE! **This is why I believe churches should grow, in relativity to the size of their communities, in such a way that they cannot be ignored.**

A BIG DEAL IN LIGHT OF ETERNITY

> *God isn't late with His promise as some measure lateness. He is restraining himself on account of you, holding back the End because he doesn't want anyone lost. He's giving everyone space and time to change.* **2 Peter 3:9 (Message)**

I can't bold and underline that statement enough! God does not want anyone to be lost. As a pastor I've had the same conversation repeatedly with people who are uncomfortable attending a large church. The statements sound something like this:

> *"I liked it better when we were all in one service."*

> *"The church is too big for me now. I was much more comfortable when it was smaller."*

> *"I get lost in this crowd. I think I need to go find a smaller church."*

In response, I have asked people a couple of questions: "What size church would you be comfortable with?" and "**How big is too big?**" Their answers are consistently somewhere between 200-400 people in attendance. This seems to be "just the right size church," where there are resources available as well as a perceived sense of momentum when the building is comfortable full. This size is also relationally manageable, granting access to leadership in addition to providing a close connection to those familiar faces in the crowd.

While I understand the responses given in regard to attending a larger church, I have to ask the bigger questions. All right then, who should we ask to leave? Should we stop having salvation invitations and baptismal services? Should we quit making a place for the thousands of people who are coming to Christ? What about the tens of thousands of people who are within a 30-minute drive of one of our locations that do not attend a church or have a real relationship with Jesus? Who will make a place for them? Who will pastor them? Who will tell them that God is not willing that they live without Him and that there is a place for them in His family? Where will they spend eternity? Are we willing to park a little further from the front door so that people can avoid hell?

I hope you are feeling the passion behind these questions. I am definitely feeling it on this side of the keyboard. As you can see, **we will never apologize for being a big church or relent on reaching as many people as possible with the message of the Gospel!**

INVESTMENTS IN LIGHT OF THE FACTS

Because Eternity is what is at stake, because Jesus gave His life up for the Church, because we are the builders of the Church in our generation and because we have been clearly commissioned, we are willing to do whatever it takes, short of sin, to accomplish the mission. All we give and invest is reasonable in light of what is at stake. I would ask you to give your time, your money, your talent, your passion, your commitment and your heart to Jesus by investing your life to build the local church. "The local church is the hope of the world."

It's a big deal to God and a big deal to us. We love the Church!

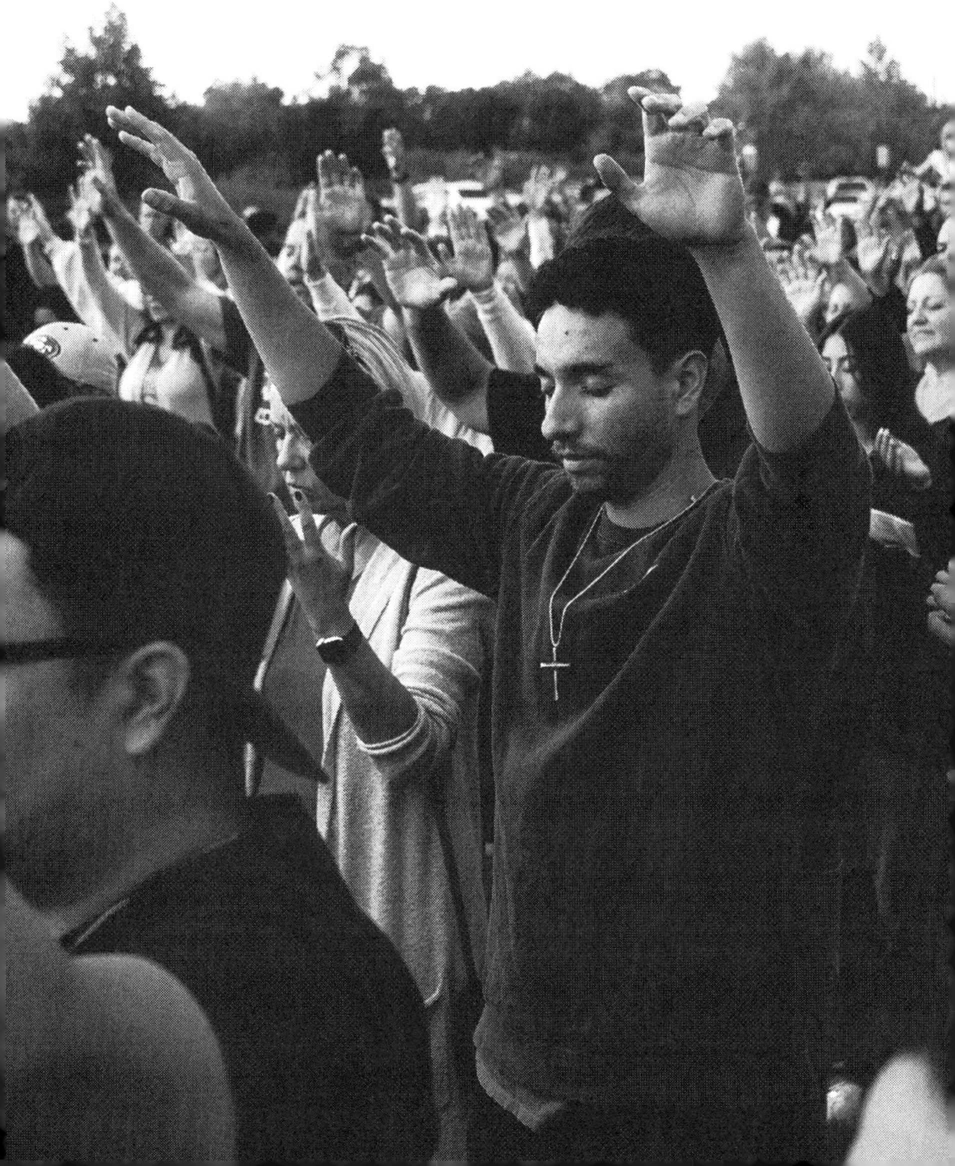

Chapter Four

BELONG

"The Church isn't a building, it's a community. We will find our significance through relationships."

Who do you belong to? What tribe are you a part of? Who is your team? Who are your people? These are questions that everyone spends a lifetime investigating, asking, struggling with and hopefully answering. One of our top ten values is that people at The Father's House would take the journey to discover where they belong and commit to the process of finding significance through relationships. This is not always an easy road, as I'm sure you're well aware, but it is worth it. Being a pastor for over thirty years now, I've attended many funerals and sat at many hospital bedsides. The most obvious and consistent element in those moments is the priority of relationships! When it's all said and done, or almost done, nothing matters but relationships. Relationships with Jesus and others are the wealth, the trophy, the prize and all that ultimately matters.

The Church has been designed by God to be a place where people connect with the Body of Christ, make meaningful friendships and find significant relationships that will last a lifetime and beyond. This is more than a biblical version of a more rewarding life; it is the difference between spiritual life and death. We truly begin to grow in our faith and our God-given gifts when we realize that we were created to be connected with others and start living that way. **Without the body of Christ we will never fully develop our true potential.** The other side of that reality is if we live disconnected other people will live in a diminished state because of what we are withholding.

Consider these verses:

> Now the body is not made up of one part but of many. If the foot should say, 'Because I am not a hand, I do not belong to the body,' it would not for that reason cease to be part of the body. But in fact God has arranged the parts in the body, every one of them, just as He wanted them to be. If they were all one part, where would the body be? As it is, there are many parts, but one body. The eye cannot say to the hand, 'I don't need you!' And the head cannot say to the feet, 'I don't need you!'
>
> **I Corinthians 12:14-15 (NIV)**

The first and most important step in belonging is to realize that I need you and you need me. We need the body, and the body needs us!

THE EVIDENCE

There are varying statistics, but all the compiled research reveals similar results indicating that over 90% of individuals who attend a new church **do not stay unless they make at least one friendship or connection in the first few weeks.** The bottom line is that people are wired for, hungry for, and in search of relationships that will last.

> "People don't care how much you know until they know how much you care"

The research proves that people will tolerate poor theology, horrible facilities, marginal communication, and a host of other ills in a church if they simply find people who care for them that they enjoy being with. The reality is this: **God created all of us with a longing for relationships; at our very core we are relational beings.** First, we are created to be in right relationship with God, then our family, then friendships and relationships in the Body of Christ that help us to grow in our faith and potential.

When we are not in a right relationship with God and the people in our world, we are not functioning at full capacity. Nobody can reach their full potential or anywhere near it, without being vitally connected with others. **1 Corinthians 12:9** tells us, *"For no matter how significant you are it is only because of what you are a part of"* (The Message). If you are well connected to the body of Christ through friendships and commitment to a local church, then I want to encourage you to stay connected and highly value it. If you are disconnected, I want to encourage you to take the steps and make the investments necessary to connect. If you are isolated, the Lord wants to draw you back into fellowship with His bride. **I don't think anyone plans on isolation; we just tend to drift toward it.** We must be intentional in identifying our isolation and moving in the other direction!

THE DANGERS OF AN ISOLATED LIFE

In **Genesis 2:18** God declared, "*It is not good for man to be alone.*" This principle and truth were not just true for Adam, but for Adam's entire race. Solitary confinement is listed among the cruelest forms of punishment because the human psyche breaks down when it is starved of connection with others. Researcher Rene Spitz showed that infants who were not held, hugged, and touched, even if someone gave them food, water, and shelter, suffered from diminished neurological development. The earliest studies of suicide showed the most predominant risk factor for those with suicidal tendencies is social isolation!

RESULTS OF AN ISOLATED LIFE

1. Loss of Perspective
When we are out of relationships there is no objective voice that helps us see things accurately and gets us back on track. We can easily get out of balance, forget we are in a battle, start making dumb decisions, and of course, if you're like me, you end up wearing the wrong clothes. Seriously, the main threat of the isolated believer is that our theology gets twisted and we become dull spiritually. The longer you stay isolated, the more you refuse wise counsel.

> *A man who isolates himself seeks his own desire; and rages against all wise judgment.*
> **Proverbs 18:1 (NKJV)**

> *As iron sharpens iron, so one person sharpens another.*
> **Proverbs 27:17 (NIV)**

2. Vulnerability to attack
Jesus repeatedly referred to us as "His sheep." As you study the characteristics of sheep you quickly realize that this label was very intentional. One of the weaknesses of sheep is that they are vulnerable to attack when they are isolated.

A wolf, mountain lion, or other predator will seldom run right into the middle of a flock to take out a single sheep, but they consistently look for those who have drifted from the group. The strength and protection of the sheep is directly connected to being with the flock and near their shepherd. To think that we can handle life without help, or that somehow, we can face the battles of life without a relational support system, is arrogance that reveals a deceived mind.

3. Fear of intimacy

People who don't have meaningful relationships tend to be more hesitant to open up because they fear rejection. The longer we live in isolation, the greater the odds become of ever building deep friendships and intimate relationships. Ultimately, we can become isolated and miss out on the greatest gifts of life! Sharing our hearts, our conversation and our lives is a learned skill that pays greater dividends as we continue to grow in it.

> *Both of us need help. I can help make your faith strong and you can do the same for me. We need each other.*
> Romans 1:12 (NLV)

4. Selfishness

As a parent and now a grandparent, I've realized that God gives us family so we can battle selfishness and learn generosity. Statistics prove that the longer a single adult stays single, the less likely it is that he or she will marry. While many individuals want companionship, there are some who become so self-sufficient and set in their ways that the thought of living a sacrificial life to serve someone else's needs becomes less appealing.

BENEFITS OF A CONNECTED LIFE

1. A more productive life!

> *Two are better than one, because they have a good return for their work.* **Ecclesiastes 4:9 (NIV)**

The return is exponential! For example, two oxen will get more than twice as much work done as one ox. You probably don't own oxen, so to put it in perspective, two creative people will create more than twice as much as one person because of creative synergism. Two people praying together will see more than twice as much return on their prayers. This is the promise of Jesus.

2. A life that recovers from failure.

> *If one falls down, his friend can help him up. But pity anyone who falls and has no one to help them up!* **Ecclesiastes 4:10 (NIV)**

Life comes complete with face-plants, inevitable falls, and failures. There is no way around it! The question is: *Will you be able to fully recover?* Will you be in proximity to the necessary encouragement, vision, strength, and perspective it requires to re-enter the race? The reality is that you are not always going to be able to pick yourself up by your own bootstraps, even though your daddy told you to do so. We need to walk together during the difficulties of life so that we do not get discouraged.

3. A life that does not grow spiritually cold!

If two lie down together, they will keep warm.
But how can one keep warm alone?
Ecclesiastes 4:11 (NIV)

An isolated heart becomes a cold heart! The soul that is alone is like the burning coal that is alone: it will grow colder rather than hotter. When we commit to living life connected, we spur one another on; we ignite passion and fire for God in one another. Hearing someone else pray, listening to a recent victory, or receiving from other people's spiritual gifts keeps the wind of the spirit blowing on the coals of our heart.

4. A life that experiences victory in spiritual battles!

Though one may be overpowered, two can defend themselves. A cord of three strands is not easily broken.
Ecclesiastes 4:12 (NIV)

The cord of three strands is a picture of two people who are walking together with Jesus at the center. His promise to us is this:

> *For where two or three are gathered together in My name, I am there in the midst of them.* **Matthew 18:20 (NKJV)**

FOUR COMMITMENTS TO LIVE LIFE CONNECTED

Let me conclude this chapter by giving you four practical ways to live in relationship and belong to something bigger than yourself.

1. Commit to a local church.
This is the biblical pattern and precedent: to be added to the local church, submit to spiritual leadership, and begin the process of building life-giving relationships in the Body of Christ. We are called out and called together as Jesus' family,

"praising God and having favor with all the people. And the Lord added to the Church daily those who were being saved" Acts **2:47 (NKJV)**. The Church is far from perfect, but it's Jesus' church and His promises are available for those who commit to His Bride!

2. Commit to being a part of a small group.

I know this might be intimidating for some and perhaps you've had some bad experiences, yet we have discovered this is the best way for people to connect and care for each other. It is here that you become the conduit of mercy, grace and resources from God to others.

You know that I have not hesitated to preach anything that would be helpful to you but have taught you publicly and from house to house. **Acts 20:20 (NIV)**

3. Commit to working through the inevitable difficulties.

Wherever you have people you will have people problems. Jesus said that offenses would come and of course, He was right. The only way we will grow is to commit to the often-difficult process of working through misunderstanding and forgiving offenses. This is usually the dividing line between those who truly grow up in God and those who pick up an offense and never get past it.

If a fellow believer hurts you, go and tell him—work it out between the two of you. If he listens, you've made a friend. **Matthew 18:15 (NIV)**

4. Commit to staying connected.

Commit to live a life of connection with the Body of Christ. Yes, times and seasons will come when it's easier to draw back, forget about the weekend gatherings, drop out of a small group and neglect to sort through offenses and misunderstandings. Yet, the only life of true growth and fulfillment is realized when we commit to fix it, sort it out, forgive, reconnect, and be an active part of the Church!

There is no biblical definition of the Church being made up of individuals who are independent and isolated. **The Church is the Body connected. It is the building built together, the family united, the flock moving as one, and the branches attached to the vine.** If you are disconnected from the Body, you are disconnected from the Savior. Any form of voluntary, independent or isolated Christianity is the result of deception or rebellion and is not God's design. Are you just dropping in to audit what God is doing in His house, or are you planted, rooted, and flourishing in the House of the Lord? We are all called as sons and daughters in unity to connect with others. It is God's desire for you to find a destination, a location and become connected in His house. Your destiny and blessing come because of obedience to this command!

> *He is like a tree planted by streams of water that yields its fruit in season, and its leaf does not wither. In all that he does, he prospers.*
> **Psalms 1:3 (ESV)**

Chapter Five

PRESENCE

"Lives flourish in God's presence. We will make a place for people to experience Him."

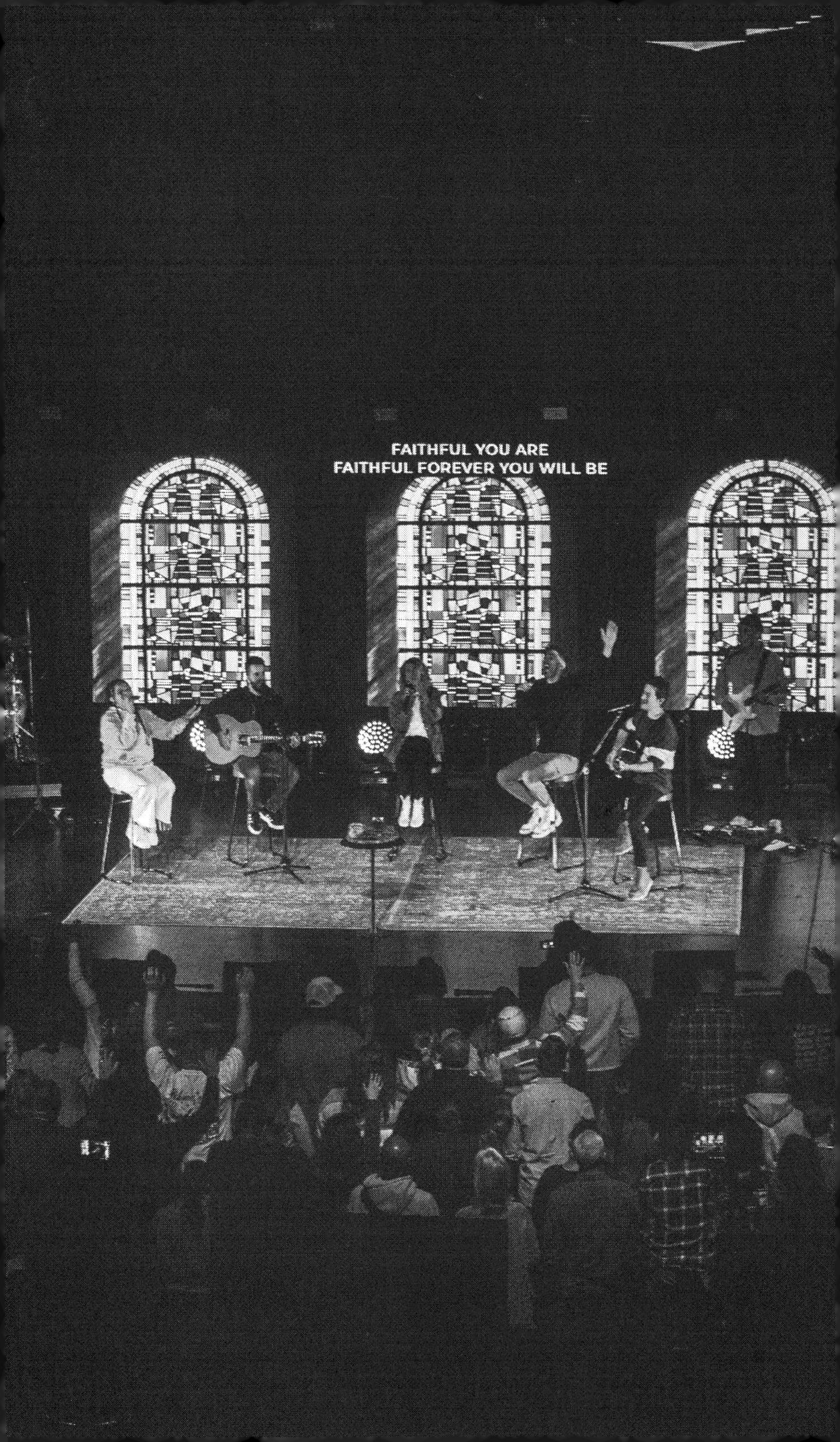
FAITHFUL YOU ARE
FAITHFUL FOREVER YOU WILL BE

Every place you go has an environment or atmosphere: shopping malls, the DMV, hospitals, theme parks, schools, homes and churches. The environment that has been created is the summation of the values, attitudes, personalities, preferences and practices of a business, organization, church, or family. These values and preferences may be stated and intentional or unidentified and compiled by default and neglect. But one thing is certain: an atmosphere and environment will be established, and the intangibles that create this atmosphere will greatly affect people's behavior.

GREAT ATMOSPHERES ARE INTENTIONAL

Whether we are talking about your favorite restaurant, your home, or your church, we need to understand that welcoming atmospheres and healthy environments don't happen accidentally. Consider Disneyland, *(not their political agendas or departure from Biblical morality in the last couple decades, but in terms of excellence and intentionality)* from the moment you get out of your car until you drag the kids away as the park closes, great attention to detail, at great expense, has been invested to create and maintain an enjoyable environment. These details can be seen from the music selections at varying decibel levels, to the placement of garbage receptacles in discrete locations. The images that are introduced as you pass from one magical land to the next join in unison with the piped-in aroma of chocolate chip cookies. All of these sounds and visuals are Disneyland's way of telling your senses, *"you love it here, don't leave, this is the happiest place on earth."*

When you walk into a home to visit someone for the first time, the atmosphere begins to say more than the conversation. The environment or "vibe" becomes very apparent. Another way to say it is that you can't hide a home full of contention with air freshener. A home that is full of love and worship will release the fragrance of God even if it's a one-room apartment in the rough part of town.

So it is with the Church. Creating an atmosphere where the presence of God is welcomed, recognized, and powerfully experienced is not accidental, it's intentional. This doesn't mean that we can control the presence of God or guarantee the Holy Spirit will be moving, but we are aware of, and intentional in, applying the biblical principles and promises regarding the atmospheres that God inhabits or avoids.

- **God inhabits** or intentionally releases His authority when the Church lifts up praises **(Psalm 22:3)**.
- The anointing, or tangible presence of the Holy Spirit, rests on believers that **gather in unity (Psalm 33)**. The other side

of this promise is the glaring absence of God's presence when churches are divided and fighting over various issues.
- The **protocol for "entering into"** the presence of God requires true worship **(Psalm 100)**.
- The Holy Spirit moves in an **atmosphere of faith and expectancy** and avoids an atmosphere of complacency and familiarity **(John 6:4-6)**.
- Heaven is an **atmosphere of perpetual worship** and
- we are commanded to pray that Heaven come to earth **(Revelation 4:8, Matthew 6:10)**.
- We have the **capability to stop the move** of the Holy Spirit (1 Thessalonians 5:19).
- God's presence abides where people are **continually seeking** Him **(Jeremiah 29:13, Deuteronomy 4:29)**.

WHAT'S IN THE HOUSE?

One of the great joys of being a pastor at The Father's House is hearing the stories of how God has consistently met with people as they enter the place of worship. This is an intangible that is bigger than all of us and really speaks of the grace of God that has caused our church to thrive. I honestly could not count how many times I've heard this similar testimony, but the amount is up into the hundreds now.

The stories sound something like this:

> "As I was walking up to the building, I felt the presence of God and was overwhelmed."

> "I cried most of the worship service for my first several visits, and I'm not a crier."

> "I encountered God in that place."

Hopefully those statements sound familiar and have been your testimony as well. I've had people call it "a good vibe," "an aura," "positive energy" and "a presence." Of course, they are all speaking of Him, not it. He is the person of the Holy Spirit that changes the atmosphere and brings heaven to earth.

THE NON-NEGOTIABLE

When we started the church in 1997 the Lord directed me to the following portion of scripture as a foundation for what He wanted to build.

The Lord replied, "My Presence will go with you, and I will give you rest." Then Moses said to Him, "If your Presence does not go with us, do not send us up from here. How will anyone know that You are pleased with me and with Your people unless You go with us? What else will distinguish me and Your people from all the other people on the face of the earth?" **Exodus 33:14-17 (NIV)**

The distinguishing element and the non-negotiable factor for Moses was the presence of God. He simply said, "God if you are not planning to go with us then I'm not going anywhere!" That has always been our philosophy of ministry, our posture of prayer, our strategy for growth and our non-negotiable ingredient for the life and future of our church. **It's all about environment and atmosphere**. It's the abiding presence, the tangible essence or nearness of God. Now I know it may sound ethereal, intangible or, super spiritual to make statements like "*we want to live in the presence of God*" or "*God was in that place*" or "*I felt God*." Let's consider how the presence of God operates in our world and in our lives.

I understand that the conversation or statement of "*God's presence being with us*" brings up several questions and concerns. Some of those questions are based on our understanding, or lack thereof, of how the Holy Spirit operates in the earth. The theological word *Pneumatology* is used to describe the operation of the Holy Spirit. The word comes from two Greek words: *pneuma*, meaning "spirit or breath", and *logy* meaning "the study of." Here is a brief look at how the Holy Spirit or presence of God operates.

THE OMNIPRESENCE

Omnipresence is an attribute of God. It's a simple yet profound truth that **God is everywhere all the time**. This attribute is solely reserved for the one true God. No other entity, spiritual force or deity has this attribute; it is reserved for God alone. The Psalmist wrote,

> *Where can I go from Your Spirit? Where can I flee from Your presence? If I go up to the heavens, You are there; if I make my bed in the depths, You are there. If I rise on the wings of the dawn, if I settle on the far side of the sea, even there Your hand will guide me, Your right hand will hold me fast. If I say, "Surely the darkness will hide me and the light become night around me," even the darkness will not be dark to You; the night will shine like the day, for darkness is as light to You.* **Psalm 139:7-12 (NIV)**

Yes, wherever you go God is there! He is in bars, strip clubs, the mall, ball games, in your living room, and in Calcutta, India, all at once. **A sobering and encouraging thought, isn't it?**

> *The eyes of the Lord are everywhere, keeping watch on the wicked and the good.* **Proverbs 15:3 (NIV)**

THE MANIFEST OR TANGIBLE PRESENCE

This is the second level of the Holy Spirit's activity that is revealed throughout the Bible and church history. The manifest presence is simply the obvious, tangible, "God is in this place" presence. The Bible describes this level of Holy Spirit in the following scriptures:

> *For where two or three gather together as My followers, I am there among them.* **Matthew 18:20 (NIV)**

> *Even as Peter was saying these things, the Holy Spirit fell upon all who were listening to the message.* **Acts 10:44 (NLT)**

> *Then when Paul laid his hands on them, the Holy Spirit came on them, and they spoke in other tongues and prophesied.* **Acts 19:6 (NLT)**

> *Be still in the presence of the Lord and wait patiently for Him to act.* **Psalm 37:7 (NLT)**

THE PERSONALIZED PRESENCE

This is the aspect of God's presence where the Holy Spirit meets with an individual, either in private or in the middle of a crowd. It can happen in a church service or when you are stuck in freeway traffic. It can be through a vision, dream, word of prophecy, audible voice, or a strong awareness of God that is accompanied by knowing what He is speaking.

> *Meanwhile, as Peter was puzzling over the vision, the Holy Spirit said to him, "Three men have come looking for you."*
> **Acts 10:19 (NIV)**

> *While they were worshiping the Lord and fasting, the Holy Spirit said, "Set apart for me Barnabas and Saul for the work to which I have called them."* **Acts 13:2 (NIV)**

While God is omnipresent (everywhere, all the time) we find that scripture teaches that His manifest and personalized presence are connected to people seeking, praying, worshiping, gathering in unity, waiting in expectancy and lifting up their voices in worship.

Our desire is to see people encounter the reality of God by experiencing His manifest and personalized presence. We don't just want people to have solid theology and sound doctrine; we want them to live in the presence. You can have all the facts and study the Bible for years and still be in a barren and miserable place, but you cannot experience the presence of God without encountering some joy and a change of perspective!

> *You make known to me the path of life; in your presence there is fullness of joy; at your right hand are pleasures forevermore.*
> **Psalm 16:11 (NIV)**

IT'S MORE THAN A FEELING

If you are a Christ follower, you no doubt love to feel the nearness of God and the power of the Spirit. We are emotional beings and encountering a living, loving God is usually an emotional event. Knowing Jesus is a relationship, and who wants to have a relationship that is void of feelings? Exactly. So, with that said we must clarify that the presence of God is a far bigger issue than how we feel or an emotional lift. There is fruit that is produced in the presence of God. When we live separated from God consequences occur because of sin or dead religious experiences that are void of His presence.

Fruit of a dead religious atmosphere:
- boredom
- disillusionment
- wrong perceptions of God
- rules without grace
- form without freedom
- bad memories of church
- idolatry
- lack of evangelism
- judgmental attitude
- comparison and spiritual pride
- spiritual barrenness
- absence of joy and strength

Fruit of being in the Presence of God
- right perspective
- joy and strength
- renewed vision
- healing
- new life and identity
- purpose and direction
- great faith
- momentum
- refreshing
- passion

- calling and commissioning
- hearing from God

Our desire is to "*make a place for people to experience Him.*" This does not mean we can conjure up the Holy Spirit or control the river of God, but the Word is clear that there are principles, steps of faith and acts of obedience that we can take to welcome the presence of God and change the atmosphere. Here are three keys to living your life in the presence of God:

1. Repent

In the book of Genesis, we see God's creation right at home and thriving in His presence. Adam and Eve enjoyed a perfect atmosphere and the continual presence of God. This is how we were originally designed, yet when they broke His commands, their immediate response was to hide from His presence.

> *And they heard the sound of the Lord God walking in the garden in the cool of the day, and Adam and his wife* **hid themselves from the presence of the Lord** *God among the trees of the garden.*
> **Genesis 3:8 (NIV)**

This account of creation is quite significant when we realize that we were designed by our creator to live in His presence. **Sin always separates!** It separates us from God, His people and eventually from those we love. When sin entered the human race through disobedience to God's Word, the process of separation continued to destroy those who were living outside the presence of God. Adam and Eve's first two sons were exposed to the power of sin, and it didn't take long for them to see the wages of sin kick in. **Genesis 4:2-16** gives the first account of rage and murder in the Bible as we read how Cain took out his younger brother. When this act of sin was carried out it had an even greater effect in creating distance between the Creator and His creation.

> *Then Cain went out from the presence of the Lord and dwelt in the land of Nod on the east of Eden.* **Genesis 4:16 (NIV)**

The "land of Nod" means the place of aimless wandering. This is also true in our lives today. When we walk away from God's presence and live for ourselves, breaking His laws and commands, we truly take up residence in the "land of aimless wandering." The only way back from that land and into the presence of God where our lives will flourish is through the cross! The Book of Hebrews tells us how access has been granted back into the presence of God.

> *And so, dear brothers and sisters, we can boldly enter heaven's Most Holy Place because of the blood of Jesus. By His death, Jesus opened a new and life-giving way through the curtain into the Most Holy Place. And since we have a great High Priest who rules over God's house, let us go right into the presence of God with sincere hearts fully trusting Him.* **Hebrews 10:19-22 (NIV)**

If you are feeling distant from God, aware that you are wandering aimlessly outside of His will for your life, or can't hear His voice, you need to return to His presence. The only place to start is the point of access that Jesus provided to the very throne room and presence. Jesus has made the way for us all, not only to be redeemed but also to live in the place we were designed to flourish. The key or door of access is through repentance: simply coming to Christ, confessing our sins and trusting His work on the cross to reconnect us to the Father so our lives will flourish!

> *Now repent of your sins and turn to God, so that your sins may be wiped away. Then times of refreshing will come from the presence of the Lord.* **Acts 3:19-20 (NLT)**

2. Feed your God-given desire for His presence.
Spiritual hunger must be fed, or it will diminish. Our appetite does not disappear, but we begin to feed our soul with substitutes that dull the desire for God and His will. Remember when you were a kid and your mom told you not to eat the cookies and ice cream before dinner? It's not that she didn't want you to have the ice cream; that is why she bought it. She simply knew that once your priority for eating was out of order, it would diminish your appetite for the things you truly needed to help you grow. **Our God-given appetite diminishes when we substitute.** We substitute time in the Word with time in front of the screen. We substitute the house of God with time at the lake or ball game. We substitute prayer time for other tasks that are vying for our precious time and attention. We lose our appetite

for His presence and begin to marginalize our spiritual health. This is a subtle process that may not be that obvious at first, but over time we will see the effects of a spirit that is being starved of the water of His presence. **We must feed our God-given desire for His Word, His house and His presence.** As we begin to feed those holy appetites, we will grow strong in the Lord and develop a lifestyle of living in the presence of God. King David talked about his desire for God's presence with these strong and passionate words.

> *One thing I have desired of the Lord, That will I seek: That I may*
> *dwell in the house of the Lord*
> *All the days of my life,*
> *To behold the beauty of the Lord, And to inquire in His temple.*
> *For in the time of trouble*
> *He shall hide me in His pavilion; In the secret place of His tabernacle*
> *He shall hide me;*
> *He shall set me high upon a rock.*
> **Psalm 27:4-5 (NKJV)**

3. Be intentional about making a place for His presence.

This requires action in response to the Word regarding how we can change the atmosphere of our homes, our churches and our communities. The Bible is filled with principles and easily applied practices that will cause us to enter into the presence of God with consistency.

Make a joyful shout to the Lord, all you lands!
Serve the Lord with gladness;
Come before His presence with singing.
Know that the Lord, He is God;
It is He who has made us, and not we ourselves; We are His people and the sheep of His pasture.
Enter into His gates with thanksgiving, And into His courts with praise. Be thankful to Him, and bless His name.
Psalm 100:1-4 (NIV)

As we enter His courts with other believers and become a community of worshipers there is an atmosphere of power, faith and love that cannot be found anywhere else. This is God's design for His body and why it is so important to be fully committed to a community of worshipping believers. When we sing at church, in small groups and at prayer meetings it's not just a warm-up time for the Word or some entertainment to get people to come to church. Our singing is one of the most frequently recorded forms of worship in the Bible. Many of the words used for singing and offering vocal praise can be overlooked until we understand the Hebrew words for praise in the Old Testament.

You are holy, enthroned on the praises of Israel.
Psalm 22:3 (NKJV)

The word "praise" in this verse is the Hebrew word *tehillah* = to lift up a song, to sing praise, a hymn or spontaneous melody of praise. This is a powerful principle and spiritual reality because

God is enthroned and comes to sit in the place of authority when His people gather to sing praise. This is why we sing out, this is why we lift our voices and make a joyful noise! When God's people sing out in faith, the atmosphere changes, the authority of God is revealed, and the Kingdom of Heaven comes to earth!

PRESENCE CHANGES EVERYTHING

Our church exists to be a place where people encounter the reality of God. This means that we will consistently give people a chance to repent and get their lives right with Jesus. We will be intentional about building a house for His presence, always looking for new ways, as well as reinforcing time-tested principles, to motivate people to stay hungry for the presence of God. Worship, the moving of the Holy Spirit and divine encounters are the highest of priorities for this house. We truly believe that one moment in the presence of God can change anything and everything. As God enlarges our heart for His house we will increasingly value investing in and building *"a place for people to experience Him."*

On a personal note: Let me encourage you to make your home a place where the presence of God will abide. Here's a list of practical ways to make your house His House:

- Frequently play worship music throughout the house
- Lift your voice and sing and pray out loud, in your home (Psa. 34:1)
- If you are musical, play your instrument as worship (Psa. 150:3-6)
- Avoid foul, demonic, and pornographic content and images in your home; (this opens the door for the demonic and grieves the Holy Spirit. 1 Thes.5:19)
- Establish a "secret place" in your home, where you consistently read the Word and pray (Psa. 91:1-2)
- Build a vocabulary of gratefulness. Take time throughout the day to speak, out loud, what you are grateful for
- Avoid arguments, foul language and raising your voice in anger. (Eph. 4:29)
- Practice speaking encouragement, compliments and positive words over your family and everyone who enters your home (Prov. 16:24)
- Make declarations over your home and those who live under your roof (Josh. 24:15)
- Ask the Holy Spirit to make himself at home every day!

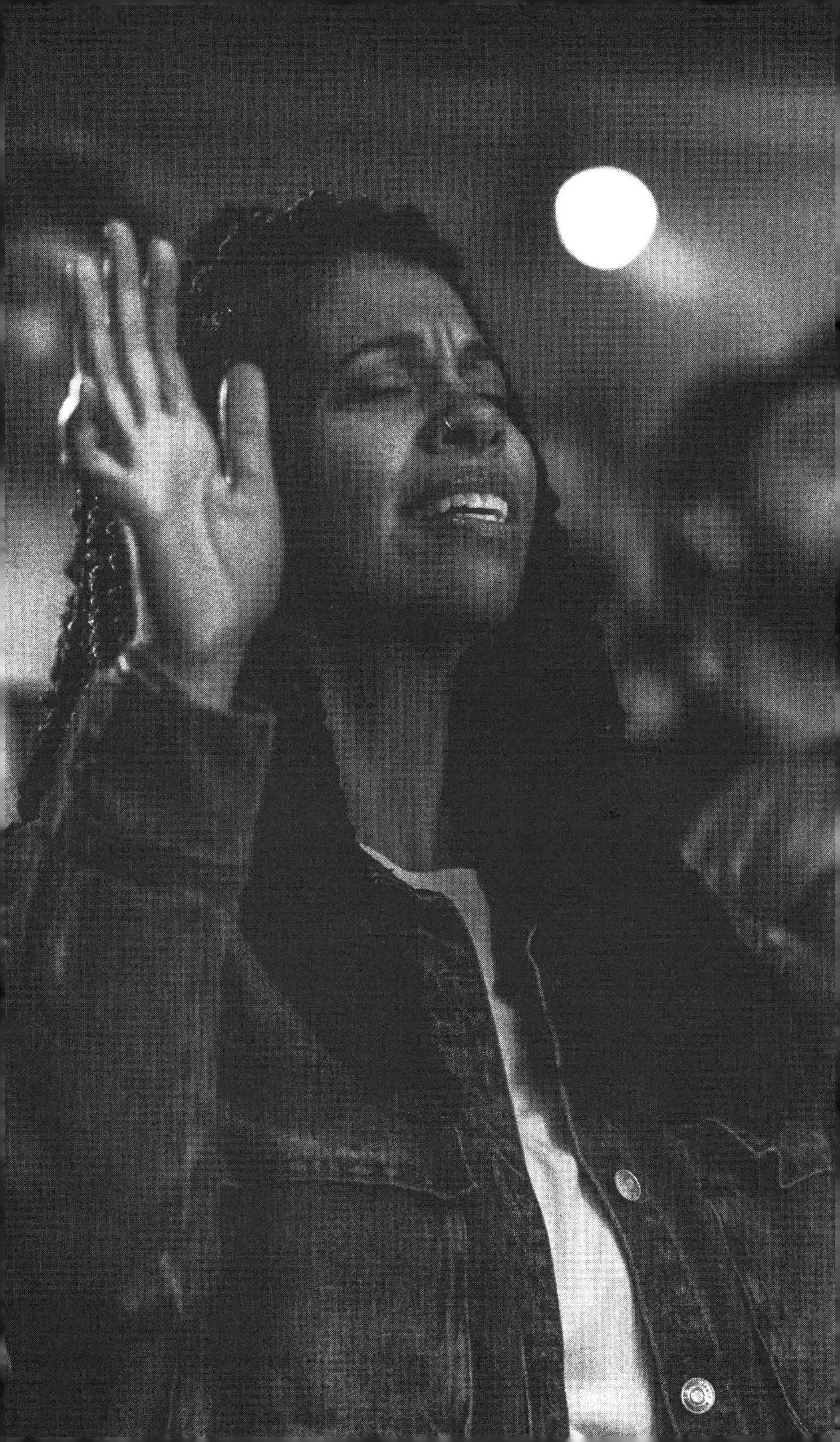

Chapter Six

GROW

"We will be life-long learners; always hearing, reading and going deeper in God's Word."

Oh, the joys of those who do not follow the advice of the wicked, or stand around with sinners, or join in with mockers. But they delight in the law of the Lord, meditating on it day and night. They are like trees planted along the riverbank, bearing fruit each season. Their leaves never wither, and they prosper in all they do.
Psalm 1:1-3 (NLT)

At this church we LOVE the Bible. We believe it is the inspired and eternal Word of God. It's not just one book, but 66 books compiled into the "canon of scripture." Over the space of 1,500 years nearly forty different authors wrote manuscripts in the form of letters, narratives, poems and sacred texts. These scrolls were preserved and divinely brought together to make up one amazing and flawless collection of writings we know today as the B-I-B-L-E.

For the word of God is alive and active. Sharper than any double-edged sword, it penetrates even to dividing soul and spirit, joints and marrow; it judges the thoughts and attitudes of the heart. Nothing in all creation is hidden from God's sight. Everything is uncovered and laid bare before the eyes of Him to whom we must give account. **Hebrews 4:12-13 (NIV)**

The Bible is unlike any other book ever written in that it's alive with the Spirit of God. If it were merely a great history book or an amazing work of fiction, wars would not have been started over it. People would not have been thrown in prison, persecuted, and given their lives to defend, distribute, and preserve it. They would not fight so hard to have it removed from schools, governments, and nations.

Yet, with every attempt to exterminate the Bible, its popularity grows. It continues to be printed in more languages and dialects while remaining at the top of the best seller lists every year! Yes, it's more than a book. It is the inspired living word of the Eternal God. The Bible also tells us that Jesus is the living word and that God has exalted His word to the highest level of authority. Those are two major reasons to be a life-long student of the scriptures.

> *In the beginning was the Word, and the Word was with God, and the Word was God. He was with God in the beginning. Through Him all things were made; without Him nothing was made that has been made.* **John 1:1-3 (NIV)**

> *For You have exalted above all things Your name and Your word.* **Psalm 138:2 (ESV)**

SUSTAINED BY THE WORD

All of us learned the same lesson back in 5th grade science class; there are two simple ingredients to survival: food and water. Without food and water, you cannot survive and, interestingly enough, **God has designed our spirit man to survive in the same manner as our flesh.** Just as our flesh cannot survive without food and water, our spirit cannot survive without spiritual food and spiritual water. The water is representative of the Holy Spirit or the presence of God. When you came to Jesus Christ and committed your life to Him you received the Holy Spirit.

> *Jesus stood and said in a loud voice, "Let anyone who is thirsty come to me and drink. Whoever believes in me, as Scripture has said, rivers of living water will flow from within them."*
> **John 7:37-38 (NIV)**

You have living water that flows within you! We also need "fresh water" or a continual renewal of the Holy Spirit in our lives. This is how we grow, flourish and overflow into our world. We stay continually "watered" through worship, coming to church and spending time with the Lord in the secret place of prayer. The WORD of GOD is the food that your spirit requires to survive! You cannot survive in the spirit if you do not have a steady diet of the WORD of GOD. **Jesus is the Living Word, and He is the Bread of Life.**

> *Jesus said, "I tell you the truth, Moses didn't give you bread from heaven. My Father did. And now He offers you the true bread from heaven. The true bread of God is the one who comes down from heaven and gives life to the world." "Sir," they said, "Give us that bread every day."*

> *Jesus replied, "I am the bread of life. Whoever comes to Me will never be hungry again. Whoever believes in Me will never be thirsty."* **John 6:32-35 (NLT)**

We need to realize what Jesus is saying here. Think back to Israel's time in the desert where manna (bread from Heaven) fell every morning. Israel was instructed to gather only enough for the day because God intended to provide for them every day. In fact, those who gathered more than their daily supply found, the next morning, that worms had eaten away at the bread, and it was no longer good for consumption. And so, every day they went out to gather their "daily bread."

God was saying, "*Yesterday's manna is not enough for today's needs so I am setting a principle into motion. Each morning go out and gather what you need for that day only.*"

Jesus says, "*I am the bread. My word is the manna from heaven. And as was the case with the manna in the desert, you need Me EVERY day.*"

Yesterday's manna will not provide enough for today's needs! Yesterday's revelation is not going to sustain you for today's trials, temptations, and challenges. If what Jesus was communicating to His followers back then is still true for His disciples today, then the ramifications are enormous. If the only time you are "*eating*" of the Word of God is during a weekend service for a few moments, you will not survive spiritually! You must have a steady diet of the Bible if you ever intend to grow and thrive, as a Christ follower! **You cannot afford to be a perpetually starving saint.**

STEADY DIET

1. Grow in Faith

So then faith comes by hearing, and hearing by the word of God.
Romans 10:17 (NKJV)

Our faith is directly connected to the Bible. Apart from this book, the WORD OF GOD, we cannot grow in our faith. We can't pray our way into greater faith, give our way into greater faith or serve our way into greater faith. FAITH COMES! Plain and simple, faith is a direct result of spending time in the Word of God.

Faith is the confidence that what we hope for will actually happen; it gives us assurance about things we cannot see.
Hebrews 11:1 (NLT)

In other words, **FAITH is the OPPOSITE of the negative REALITY that I'm facing.** As we spend time studying and meditating on the scriptures, we see how God works in the lives of His people and we begin to believe that He will do the same in our lives. The words and principles begin to come alive in our hearts and we grow in confidence that God will do what He says He will do! This is the net result of spending time in the Word. This is the substance of faith.

2. Grow in Grace

> *Husbands, love your wives, just as Christ also loved the church and gave Himself for her, that He might sanctify and cleanse her with the washing of water by the word, that He might present her to Himself a glorious Church, not having spot or wrinkle or any such thing, but that she should be holy and without blemish.*
> **Ephesians 5:25-27 (NLT)**

The word of God **washes** us and **cleanses** us. It removes the spot and the stain of sin and makes us HOLY before God.

The WORD says in **Romans 8:1**, "*There is no condemnation for those who are in Christ Jesus.*"

The WORD says in **Psalm 103:12**, "*As far as the east is from the west I have removed your transgressions.*"

The WORD says in **Isaiah 1:18**, "*Though your sins are like scarlet, they shall be as white as snow.*"

As we read, meditate on and listen to the preaching of the Word, our spirits are washed, and we receive grace for the day. Instead of walking around feeling weak and condemned, we are strengthened and walk in the reality of the continued work of God's grace in our lives.

3. Grow in Victory

I have hidden Your word in my heart, that I might not sin against You.
Psalm 119:11 (NLT)

David is saying, "*I have hidden the word of God in my heart so that when temptation comes, when the ability to 'sin against God' comes, I have the weapons necessary, hidden in my heart, to fight the fight so that I don't fall into temptation.*"

A "sin problem" always starts as a temptation problem. You don't start out with a cussing, lying, anger, or lust addiction. Those sins are the result of our inability to battle temptation in its infancy stages. Then, through perpetual yielding to the temptation and pattern of sin, it becomes a stronghold in our lives. We often fail in our attempts to overcome temptation. We get frustrated with ourselves because we think that if we try harder, get some more accountability, or feel bad enough, that we'll do better next time, but next time produces the same results.

The answer to a victorious life is not to try to quarantine ourselves from temptation, although wisdom cries out to not set ourselves up for failure. The key to victory is through faith in the redemptive work of Jesus Christ, having the Word of God hidden in our heart, and daily applying the Word to all areas of our life. Instead of a theology of avoidance we begin to realize that **confronting temptation and spiritual battles with the residing Word of God is the only way to sustained victory.**

PRACTICAL APPLICATION

Most of what I've been sharing in this chapter is common knowledge and probably review for you. The real power is found in the practical application of these truths. Let me give you three ways, or application points, that will cause you to be strong in the Word and live in continuous victory as you commit to an **"always lifestyle."**

1. Always Hearing

This simply means come to church and hear the preaching and teaching of the Word. Continually listen to good sermons and teaching podcasts. Have the Word of God flowing into your mind through the receptacle of your ears! **Prioritize the biblical mandate to hear your pastors proclaim the Word of God.**
It may not always be as exciting as you hoped or a topic you would have chosen, but over the long haul, you will grow strong through the process of consistently being fed and challenged by the Word.

All the believers devoted themselves to the apostles' teaching, and to fellowship, and to sharing in meals and to prayer.
Acts 2:42 (NLT)

2. Always Reading

Commit to a daily Bible reading plan. Go online to tfh.org/read and you will find an easy application where you can choose a reading plan that works for you. If you get behind or fall off the plan, don't worry about it too much. Don't condemn yourself or quit. Simply jump back in and start reading your daily portions again.

I would also encourage you to supplement your Bible reading plan with some great Christian books that will inspire you and give you insight into particular areas. I won't list titles here, but feel free to ask one of our staff pastors or your small group leader, regarding the right book for the season you are going through.

3. Always Going DEEPER

I've been reading and studying the Bible for over 40 years, and it feels like I am just getting started! There is an ocean of revelation and truth to dive into and we will never exhaust the depths of the Word, so go deeper! Some practical ways to do that are:

- Begin to use some study tools (easily accessed online).
- Attend a Bible study small group.
- Consider becoming a Leadership College student (age

appropriate).
- Attend the Biblical Studies Program, provided at the church.
- Attend conferences and seminars (both at your home church and other venues).
- Find people farther down the road than you and ask them to help you go deeper in the Word.

DON'T GET SIDETRACKED

A great temptation for those who are determined to keep growing in the Word is to get caught up inside roads of revelation and random questionable doctrines that really don't produce growth or make us more like Jesus. My advice to you would be to **stay away from splitting theological hairs with people who are looking for a doctrinal argument**.

As a church we do not get caught up in peripheral scriptural arguments when it comes to preaching and teaching during our gatherings. A strong passage of scripture regarding those who are causing division over doctrinal minutia can be found in the book of Titus.

This is a faithful statement of what we believe. Concerning this, I want you to put it out there boldly so that those who believe in God will be constant in doing the right things, which will benefit all of us. Listen, don't get trapped in brainless debates; avoid competition over family trees or pedigrees; stay away from fights and disagreements over the law. They are a waste of your time. If a person is causing divisions in the community, warn him once; and if necessary, warn him twice. After that, avoid him completely...
Titus 3:8-10 (VOICE)

There are only two times in the New Testament where God tells us to avoid people completely and one of those times is in reference to "brainless debates" over scripture.

Clearly, we are going to fight for truth and not back down in regard to what we would view as "non-negotiable" foundational doctrines of our faith. This includes the inerrancy of scripture, the Trinity, Jesus being fully God and fully man, virgin birth, bodily resurrection of Christ, water baptism, Lord's Supper, judgment, an eternal Heaven, and Hell, and so on. We have determined that we will not become drawn into arguments that have caused division in the body of Christ for years, even though there are still strong points of view on both sides of the issues. Yes, we will study, have an opinion and back our opinion with the Word of God, but there are many subjective areas of scripture that I believe are not worth arguing over, dividing, or wasting time trying to defend or promote. Some of the debates that have caused division in the Body of

Christ for years include:

- End time events and timelines
- Should women be in ministry?
- What day should we attend church?
- Dress code and dietary concerns for Christians
- Worship styles, music preferences – traditional vs. contemporary
- Eternal security vs. apostasy

…and on and on they go. I'm not saying we shouldn't study these topics and many more that fall into this category. I believe we should be aware of the arguments and understand the different views and opinions that are out there. For example, we believe that women should be in ministry and allowed to preach and teach. We just don't believe that arguing with denominations and churches, that are dead set against it, will ever produce good fruit. Don't get caught up in defending or attacking an interpretation of scripture that will end up being a no-win argument or a subjective conclusion at best.

Keeping it simple does not equate to being simple. It is actually wisdom to stay focused on Jesus and His clear instructions on how to live. The Apostle Paul said,

> *I claimed to know nothing with certainty other than the reality that Jesus is the Anointed One, the Liberating King, who was crucified on our behalf.* **1 Corinthians 2:2 (VOICE)**

Make the determination that you will be a life-long learner. If you have become stagnant in your Word life or feel that you have reached a plateau in your knowledge of God, then take this as a challenge to relaunch into a personal campaign to go deeper. If you've stalled out, jump back into your daily Bible reading program, join a study small group, and dive into some good books that will stir your faith. Show up every weekend at church for the preaching of the Word and start growing again! Without faith you cannot please God and there is only one way to get faith—hearing what God is saying through His Word.

Chapter Seven

GENEROSITY

"We will lead the way with irrational generosity. We truly believe it is more blessed to give than to receive."

If you take a moment to consider some of the great people in history you will quickly find a common denominator: they were all generous people. They lived for others and not for themselves as they showed the world what a life well lived looked like by exemplifying radical generosity. One famous figure, Mother Teresa, gave up her future as an up and coming leader in the Catholic Church in order to serve some of the most devastated people on the planet in Calcutta, India. When asked why she chose this lifestyle of serving the lepers and the hungry, she replied,

> "A life not lived for others, is not a life." **– Mother Teresa**

The Apostle Paul is another great man of God who lived to give it all away. The history of his life and his writings make it quite clear that he was living for the bigger picture and willing to give everything to see others find life in Christ. As he set sail from one of his final church plants some of his last words were regarding generosity.

> *This is my last gift to you, this example of a way of life: a life of hard work, a life of helping the weak, a life that echoes every day those words of Jesus our King, who said, 'It is more blessed to give than to receive'.* **Acts 20:35 (Voice)**

Consider the words of Jesus,

> *The Son of Man did not come to be served, but to serve, and to give His life as a ransom for many.* **Matthew 20:28 (NIV)**

There is no doubt the life of Jesus is the embodiment of this message of radical and irrational generosity. Biblical generosity is refreshing, inspiring and readily available to all of us.

Generosity is also the road to prosperity. That's not a "give to get" message. It is simply a scriptural and spiritual reality clearly spelled out in the Word of God. I would ask you to lay aside your doctrinal bias or any overreactions to imbalanced teaching and simply read through the scriptures to see what they clearly say about this subject of giving and receiving.

> *Give freely and become more wealthy; be stingy and lose everything; The generous will prosper; those who refresh others will themselves be refreshed.*
> **Proverbs 11:24-25 (NLT)**

In our value statement we make the commitment that we will live with **"irrational generosity."** This means simply living the life of a giver in a way that doesn't make sense to the logical mind. This is the definition of Biblical stewardship and generosity. Think about it. God says if you want more, give what you have away. If you want to live under the blessing of God, give the first tenth of your income back to Him, then give some more and you will receive such a blessing that "*you will not have room to contain it*" **(Malachi 3:10)**. Those who give will have more and those who hang on to all they acquire will have less. That doesn't make sense to human reasoning; it's illogical, it's irrational, yet it's eternal truth.

Our church was founded and has grown under the blessing of the Lord because of irrational generosity. Now, before I list a few instances of that generosity, let me give you this disclaimer: these facts and numbers are not a boast in how great we are but simply the best way I can explain how this works and boast about the faithfulness of God. The motivation for our irrational generosity is faith and the reality that we are continually in need of God's provision. We know His promise is to take what we give and multiply it; to open heaven when we give the first and the best, providing more resources as we give what's in our hand. **The conclusion is that we can't afford not to give!**

At the writing of this book The Father's House just gave away over $2.8M in the last calendar year to various ministries, mission works, and community projects. We will probably exceed that amount next year and in the years to come. In a time where the economy has been a real roller coaster of inflation and interest rates, this is not a rational way of thinking for a church that needs to raise millions of dollars for a new building projects! Yet, it makes perfect sense when we walk by faith.

The first day our church started on March 2, 1997, there was just over $5,000 given in the very first offering and we gave it all away to missions and other ministries. That is quite illogical when you consider the fact that we had no money, no supporting organization backing us and I was unemployed. God challenged us to sow the "tithe," the first and the best from our new church and trust Him for the future. I'm sure glad we did!

A few years ago a church across town was in the middle of a building project. The bank had pulled their financing and it looked as if the project was going to be shut down indefinitely. After some prayer and meeting with our leaders, we decided to take all of our weekend offerings and give it to this local church to inspire them and hopefully get them restarted. This means we took over 25% of our monthly income and gave it away.

On that great weekend our church gave $135,000 in tithes and offerings and we took the entirety of it and presented it to this local church. Up until that point in the history of our church we had never had that large of a weekend offering, not even close... ever! It seemed illogical to give it away, but not to GOD! Oddly enough, after that history-making weekend the amount we sowed into another church became the new water mark for our weekly finances and we never went below that number again. Crazy how that works!

Another area where we have stepped out in faith is taking responsibility for the hungry and hurting people in our cities. A few years ago we purchased a Goodyear tire store and converted it into the Vacaville Storehouse. We never intended to sell product or take money from anyone. This may seem irrational, but we are convinced that all of our community outreach programs in Vacaville, Napa, East Bay, Roseville, Calgary Canada and all the cities where there is a TFH plant, not only fulfill the commands of Jesus but they continue to keep us under an "open heaven" as a church and organization. This is a fact. Every year that we give more away, our budget and yearly income increases. This is irrational and illogical, but it is God's economy at work!

> *Blessed are those who are generous, because they feed the poor.* **Proverbs 22:9 (NLT)**

> *If you help the poor, you are lending to the Lord— and He will repay you!* **Proverbs 19:17 (NLT)**

Time after time when there have been floods, tsunamis and earthquakes around the world, I have seen our church step up and in a spontaneous moment give tens of thousands of dollars to people they have never seen. It's illogical, yet it is the road to a blessed life and a blessed church! **We will never draw back from radical, irrational generosity.** Generosity is our way of initiating the flow of divine resources that God wants to pour through us. **When you become the resource for others then God makes sure more resource comes to you!** The generous person will always have something to give away. In other words, **God is committed to resourcing the "resourcers."** As it is written,

> *'He has scattered abroad His gifts to the poor; His righteousness endures forever.' Now He who supplies seed to the sower and bread for food will also supply and increase your store of seed and will enlarge the harvest of your righteousness. You will be made rich in every way so that you can be generous on every occasion, and through us your generosity will result in thanksgiving to God.*
> **2 Corinthians 9:9-11 (NIV)**

I love those verses. They are so clear and concise that it's really hard to interpret them wrong. Bottom line, God wants us to live with an open hand, be generous all the time and watch Him pour the increase into our lives. Of course, this life of faith and prosperity will be tested and we have to fully commit to trusting God and not our own strength. For those who take this path of trust and live life as a giver, you will never want to turn back!

> *Remember this—a farmer who plants only a few seeds will get a small crop. But the one who plants generously will get a generous crop. You must each make up your own mind as to how much you should give. Don't give reluctantly or in response to pressure. For God loves the person who gives cheerfully. And God will generously provide all you need. Then you will always have everything you need and plenty left over to share with others.*
> **2 Corinthians 9:6-8 (NLT)**

GOD'S COMMITMENT TO THE GENEROUS

As a pastor I seem to be in a spot where I get to help people adjust their theology from time to time. I've heard plenty of people quote the following verse without connecting it to the context of the generous life, which is what the entire chapter is about.

> *And my God will meet all your needs according to the riches of His glory in Christ Jesus.* **Philippians 4:19 (NIV)**

Let me give you the good news first. This promise is 100% true and you can bank your life on it. Now, here is the bad news for some. This promise is reserved for the givers, the generous and those who support the ministries that God has commissioned. The context of this verse is the apostle Paul speaking to the Church in Philippi. He is thanking them for their consistent and generous giving as they financially supported him while he continued to plant churches. Paul told them that even when other churches slowed down in their support, the Church in Philippi kept giving. He closes out the letter by saying, "And my God shall supply..."

Generosity goes far beyond giving our money. Although there is an abundance of scriptures that deal with our finances, our treasure, our investments and the love of money, the principles of generosity work in many areas of our lives.

Because generosity is an issue of the heart it means that all of us are candidates to live in the blessing of God, to see increase in our lives and to invest what we have to make others' lives more valuable, no matter our hourly wage or yearly income.

GOD'S PROMISE OF PROSPERITY

Biblical prosperity is the condition of living under the tangible blessing of God. This tangible blessing includes but is not limited to financial increase. The various translations of the Bible use words like "abundance, increase and multiply" to describe this state of blessing. This is the promise we stand on and the application of a biblical covenant that applies to us in regard to "divine prosperity."

> *So you are all children of God through faith in Christ Jesus. And all who have been united with Christ in baptism have been made like Him. There is no longer Jew or Gentile, slave or free, male and female. For you are all Christians—you are one in Christ Jesus. And now that you belong to Christ, you are the true children of Abraham. You are His heirs, and now all the promises God gave to him belong to you.* **Galatians 3:26-29 (NLT)**

If we truly believe that the covenant of blessing God made with Abraham is ours in Christ, then we should expect to experience prosperity in our lives for the purpose of blessing the nations.

Prosperity is never about us amassing more wealth and stuff for the sake of consuming it. We are "blessed to be a blessing" to all the nations of the earth. If you study all the places in the Bible where God introduced and confirmed His covenant with His people, you will see that health, wealth, land, influence and abundance are inseparable from the covenant. The frequent misapplication or false teaching on this subject usually includes the idea that God simply wants us to have more stuff because He loves us. Yes, He loves us and He wants to prosper us, but it's not for us to heap up and consume for ourselves. The accurate interpretation and application of the prosperity message must be based on the premise that God has called us to be a blessing to other people and nations.

Biblical Prosperity: "Having all you need and some to give away."

Generosity is not a financial position, it is a heart condition!

We can be generous or stingy with many things in our lives: our talent, our time, our affections, our possessions, our smiles, hugs and a long list of other resources that we are managing while on this earth. Let me encourage you to live a life of generosity. If you are on that path don't look back or diminish your faithful giving. If you have not stepped out in faith and begun the journey of generosity, please start now!

Don't waste this precious life consuming all you have been given and spending all your energy and resources on yourself.

Your heavenly father is just waiting for you to open the door of His unlimited resources as you make a determination to live a generous life. God is waiting for a reason to bless your business and finances beyond what you have ever imagined! So let's give God plenty of reasons to get supernaturally involved in our lives.

God has a big plan and a big world waiting for those who choose the way of generosity!

"The world of the generous gets larger and larger; the world of the stingy gets smaller and smaller." **Proverbs 11:24 (The Message)**

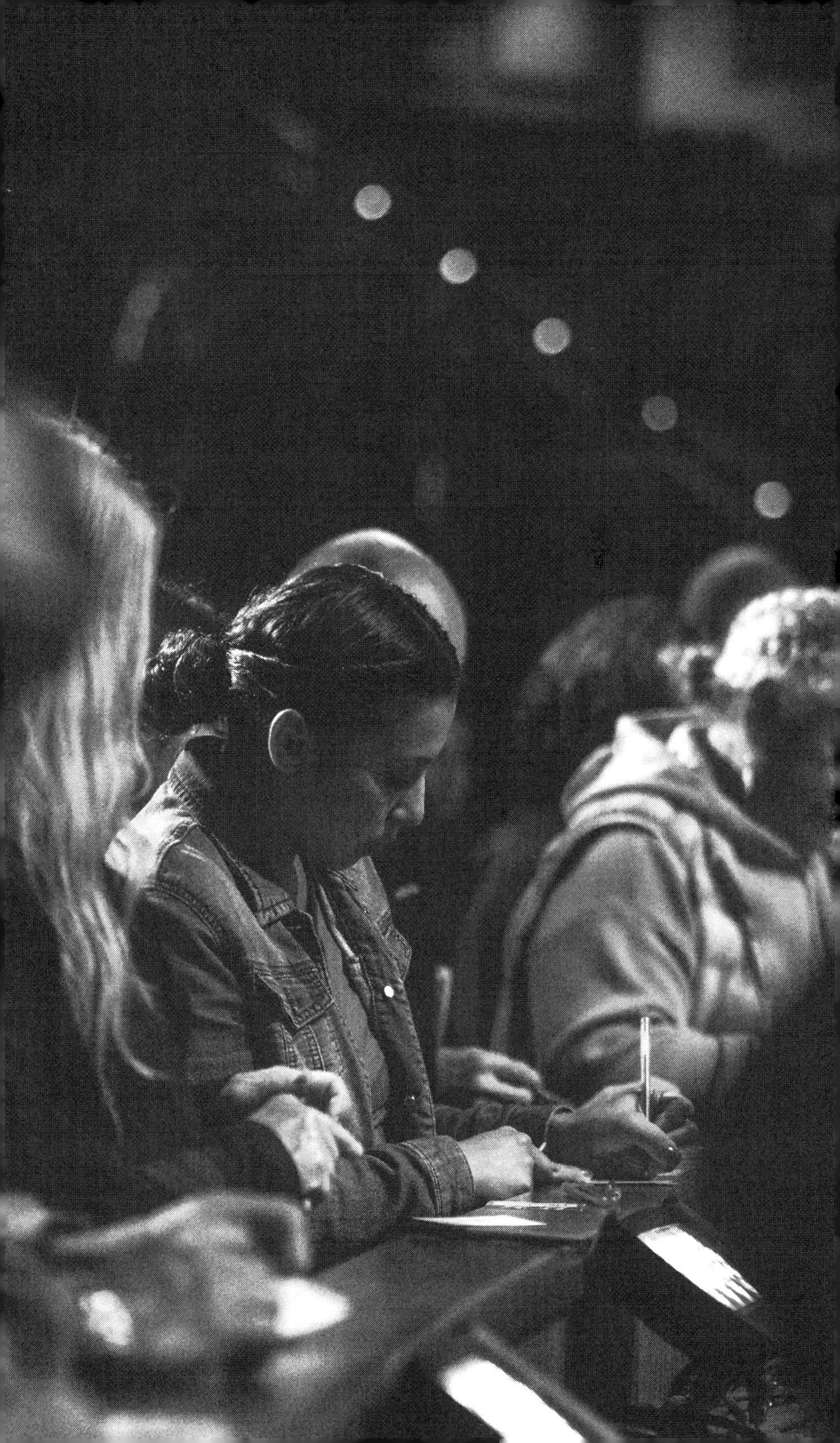

Chapter Eight

"We will always bring our best, honoring God and inspiring people."

EXCELLENCE

Think about a time when you experienced excellence and it made a serious and lasting impression on you. Remember the first time you went to a high-end resort or hotel? How about a concert where the sound, lighting, production and talent level was far beyond what you had experienced at prior events?

Perhaps you still remember and talk about a restaurant where the food, ambiance and service was so well executed that you were stunned. Yes, those are the lasting effects of being impacted by excellence. Conversely, really bad experiences create negative opinions and mediocre experiences are forgettable, but excellence leaves a lifelong and often life-changing impression.

> *"Excellence is something people feel."* **– Disney Corporation**

While we want people's experience in the House of God to be unforgettable, our motivation for highly valuing excellence is not so that we can impress people and therefore hold an unforgettable place in their memory banks. Instead, our motivation for bringing God our best and exemplifying excellence is simply because **excellence is who God is and how we can best represent Him to the world.** Having been raised in church as a pastor's kid, I've seen the other side of excellence. There are plenty of mediocre, forgettable, under-budgeted, below average and embarrassing representations of the King and His Kingdom. I have always had a strong conviction that this is not the Biblical image that God intended or desired His Church to aspire to. Sadly, when the Church places little value on producing atmospheres of excellence and serving people with a spirit of excellence as we represent the character of God to the world, unbelievers may be led to the conclusion that Christianity must not be a big deal or worth giving up their lives for. The Bible tells us that God is excellent and that everything He does is excellent.

> *Sing to the Lord, for He has done excellent things; Let this be known to all the world.* **Isaiah 12:5 (NKJV)**

> *Praise Him for His mighty acts;*
> *Praise Him according to His excellent greatness!*
> **Psalm 150:2 (NKJV)**

Other translations use synonyms for excellence such as: immense greatness, incredible greatness, unequaled greatness and the abundance of His greatness. All of these words describe the character of God and how He operates. He is over the top, extravagant, pays attention to detail and goes beyond our expectations. My conviction is that those who are called to follow and be like Him should aspire to be like Him in every way, modeling His attributes of excellence in every aspect of their lives! Excellence is also a word used to describe the way God rules over His people with majesty and power.

> *Ascribe strength to God; His excellence is over Israel, And His strength is in the clouds.* **Psalm 68:34 (NKJV)**

This simply means that God does things at the highest level. Through the way He interacts with His creation and displays His glory, the attributes of His character are revealed. This is why doing life and ministry with a spirit of excellence is directly connected to revealing the character of God. God never does anything half way, half hearted, good enough or satisfactory. His ways and acts are always excellent, above and beyond, filled with glory and revealing His nature.

Excellence = Doing the best you can with **what you have. An excellent Spirit** = Living above mediocrity and **giving your best.**

This phrase, "an excellent spirit," is from the Book of Daniel and describes his heart and attitude. His life and behavior surpassed those around him; his character was above and beyond. The phrase "a spirit of excellence" is also used to describe something or someone who is operating in a realm that surpasses the normal or expected.

Our value at The Father's House says that "*We will bring our best.*" This is the behavior and distinctive lifestyle of those who have an excellent spirit. God is not judging us based on someone else's talents and abilities. Neither is He requiring a level of performance, behavior or financial investment that we are incapable of. What this means is that **everyone can live with a spirit of excellence and embrace this value!** What does excellence look like in your life and where can you see yourself moving from mediocrity to excellence? Is it your attitude and passion level at work? Perhaps in the way you are taking care of your home and how you maintain and care for the material goods that you possess? Is it evident in how you raise your children and invest in your marriage? Are you developing the gifts and talents in your life? How about your finances and the way you serve at your church? You see, the principle of bringing our best applies in every area of our lives, and approaching life with a spirit of excellence changes everything.

Because of Who God is "*we will bring our best, honoring God and inspiring people.*"

King David had messed up in **2 Samuel Chapter 24** and God required a sacrifice in order to make things right. As King David headed off to present this offering to the Lord, a fellow by the name of Araunah saw the king and his entourage approaching his home to purchase a field. When Araunah was asked if he would sell a piece of his land to accommodate the sacrifice, he replied, "*Take it, it's yours. You are the king! There is no charge.*" In response to that statement David made a reply that revealed his heart and the character of God:

> *But [King David] replied to Araunah, "No, I insist on buying it, for I will not offer to the Lord that which cost me nothing."*
> **Samuel 24:24 (NIV)**

This is a great Old Testament story that reveals a pervasive biblical truth. **God is always worth our first and our best, simply because of who He is!** This is really the bottom line of the tithing principle. Tithing, which means 10%, was never about putting a financial burden on God's people or God trying to set up a way to finance the mission of the Church. At the core of the tithing principle is the truth that spans all of time and history, both Old and New Testament alike. **God requires the first and the best because that is simply who He is and what He deserves.** To bring Him second best, the leftovers, or a mediocre effort while serving Him, actually falls under the category of robbing God of what is due His name.

OUR COMMITMENT

As a church we have determined to carry out life and ministry with a spirit of excellence. **We will always bring our best because this is one of the main ways we can reflect the nature and character of God.** When I sing with all of my heart, give the first and the best, create to the fullest capacity of my ability, serve with passion, lead with diligence, love with abandon and never stop short of what I know is my best, I am honoring God and inspiring people.

I want to challenge you to live your life with this value of excellence. Remember, "*If it's worth doing, it's worth doing well.*" Never settle for your average performance or try to just get by with the bare minimum. Let's inspire the people in our lives as they watch us live with a spirit of excellence! Paul's prayer for the Church is my prayer for you as well.

> *And this I pray, that your love may abound still more and more in knowledge and all discernment, that you may approve the things that are excellent, that you may be sincere and without offense till the day of Christ.* **Philippians 1:9-11 (NKJV)**

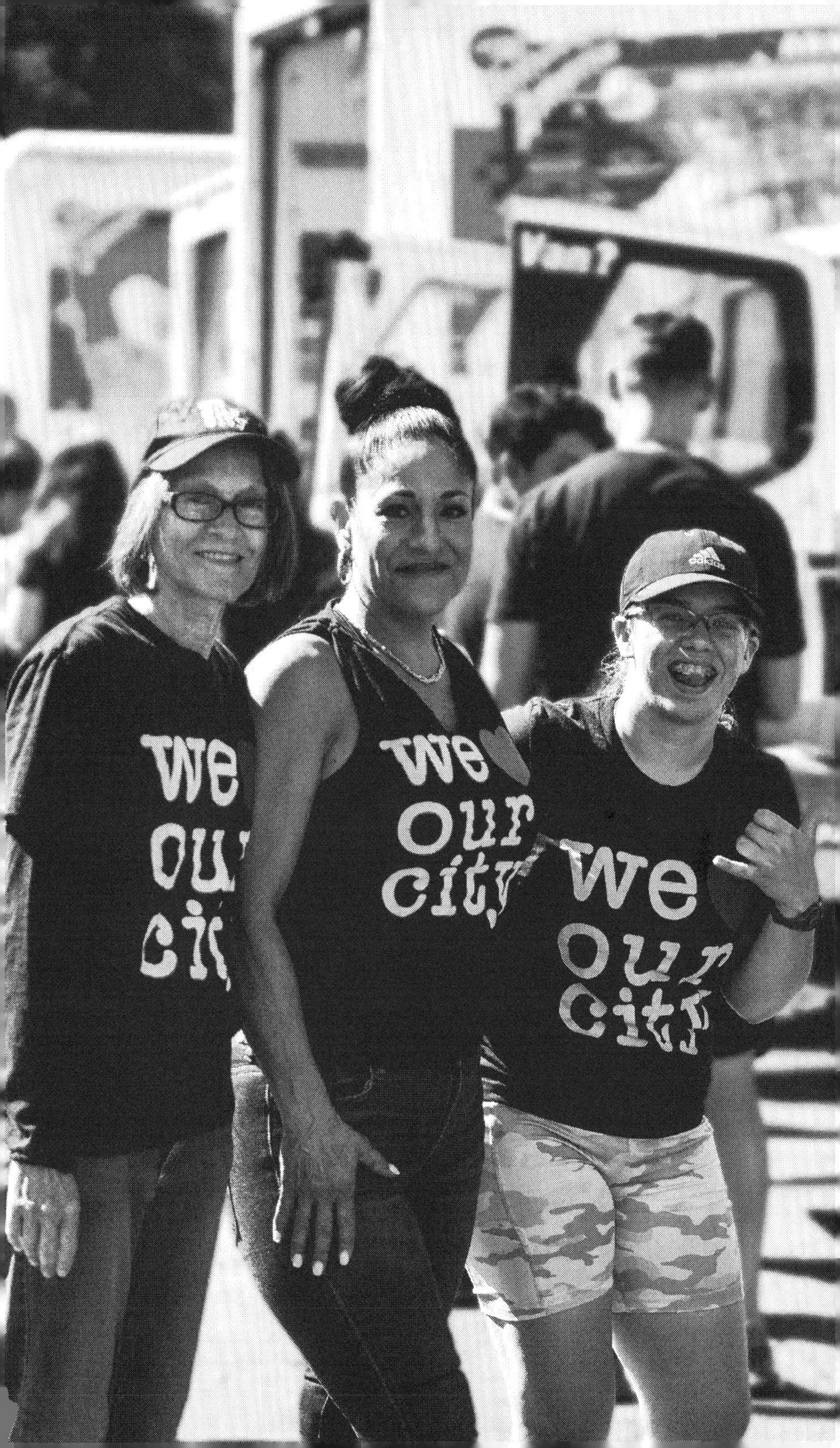
we
our

Chapter Nine

OUR CITY

"Actions speak louder than words. We love our city and will take responsibility for it."

Jesus never intended for His Church to end up being a few people hidden away in old buildings that nobody really noticed or cared about. When He said, "I will build my Church" (Matthew 16:18) and "Go and make disciples of all nations" (Matthew 28:19), Jesus envisioned a Church that would impact every nation, region and city with undeniable power and irresistible love. Jesus told us that His Church would be an overcoming Church, obvious, unavoidable and the epicenter of light and hope for every community.

> *You are the salt of the earth. But what good is salt if it has lost its flavor? Can you make it salty again? It will be thrown out and trampled underfoot as worthless. You are the light of the world— like a city on a hilltop that cannot be hidden. No one lights a lamp and then puts it under a basket. Instead, a lamp is placed on a stand, where it gives light to everyone in the house. In the same way, let your good deeds shine out for all to see, so that everyone will praise your heavenly Father.* **Matthew 5:13-16 (NLT)**

THE TANGIBLE LOVE OF JESUS

The Word is very clear and consistent in revealing what true faith looks like; it is obvious, tangible, and quantifiable. Faith takes action, faith serves, faith gives, faith helps, and faith reaches and rescues. **If it does not have tangible evidence or results, then it's not real faith!** The Father's House is a church that cannot be ignored because of the way we live out our faith through loving and caring for people.

> *What good is it, dear brothers and sisters, if you say you have faith but don't show it by your actions? Can that kind of faith save anyone? Suppose you see a brother or sister who has no food or clothing, and you say, 'Good-bye and have a good day; stay warm and eat well'—but then you don't give that person any food or clothing. What good does that do? So you see, faith by itself isn't enough. Unless it produces good deeds, it is dead and useless. Now someone may argue, 'Some people have faith; others have good deeds.' But I say, 'How can you show me your faith if you don't have good deeds? I will show you my faith by my good deeds.' You say you have faith, for you believe that there is one God. Good for you! Even the demons believe this, and they tremble in terror. How foolish! Can't you see that faith without good deeds is useless?*
> **James 2:14-20 (NLT)**

I can't say it any better or straighter than the Book of James. "*Faith without good deeds is dead and worthless*" **(James 2:14-26)**. Our faith must result in the tangible evidence that Jesus loves people or it's not real. People will recognize the difference. When someone is hungry, they don't need to hear a sermon until they have had something to eat. When someone is cold, they don't need to be taught a Bible lesson until they are given a coat and a blanket. When children have no place to go after school, no sports programs, no mentors, and no hope for a future, they need more than a church service. They need the obvious and tangible love of Jesus being expressed through His church in ways that see and meet their immediate needs.

At The Father's House, we have determined that we will be the evidence of a loving God in our cities. Yes, it's time consuming, expensive, and often exhausting. Yet, this is what faith looks like in public. God has not called us to preach to our cities until we have first served our cities. God has not called us to have services for those who are saved and doing well, while the hurting stay on the streets or behind closed doors. Far too often the Church is serving the saved and blessing the blessed while the world is waiting to see Jesus through our acts of kindness. People need the tangible love of Jesus! They need a hug, a doughnut, a sweater, a bag of groceries and a chance to receive from Him with no expectation of return—no strings attached.

TAKING RESPONSIBILITY

A few years ago, when I was praying about the future of our church, I asked the Lord to give us more spiritual authority in our cities. As I prayed, I felt the Spirit drop this statement in my heart:

If you want more authority, simply take more responsibility.
As I digested that powerful thought my whining conversation was brought to an abrupt halt. You can apply this statement to almost any leadership or spiritual endeavor and it makes perfect sense. If you want more authority in your business, such as advancement, it means that you will have to take on more responsibility. If you want increased authority over a team, it means that you will have to become a team leader or the coach. God entrusts more authority to those who are being faithful with what they currently have and are willing to take on more responsibility, not those who are critical of the current effectiveness while being resistant to take on more responsibility.

Several years ago, I was on a trip to Tokyo speaking at a worship conference, and God spoke to me clearly in sentence form. This is a rare occurrence for me, and it had my full attention. During this mission trip, I was praying for Northern California and all that God was doing through The Father's House. Although I don't understand why, over the years I've noticed that I hear from God about our church much more clearly when I'm far away. Consequently, in that moment of prayer I was asking God to "*take us to the next level, send revival and show me what to do to see His promises fulfilled in our church.*"

The Lord responded, "I*f you don't start taking more responsibility for the physical needs of the people in your city, the church will become progressively more irrelevant to your community.*"

That was a wake-up call! I knew exactly what He was referring to and had a pretty good idea of how we could take more responsibility for our cities. When I returned from that trip, our leadership team began looking for a building to expand our benevolence ministries and discussing ways that we could begin serving our city. In the past, we had always given away food and resources to hurting people around the holidays, but this was a "whole nutha level!" In 2007, we invested $1.4 million to purchase and renovate a Goodyear tire store into the Vacaville Storehouse. About the same time God brought Pastors Raymond and Kim, our community outreach pastors, to join our staff. For over fifteen years, our community service outreach has grown exponentially. Through feeding programs, Adopt-a-Block, and a variety of ministries that take place every week, we are seeing hundreds of members invest their time and finances to serve our city, and I don't see it slowing down anytime soon!

THE MOTIVATION MUST BE LOVE

How do we love our city? We pray for it! That's the starting point and the catalyst that will spark an ongoing desire to serve our city and see it prosper. There is a familiar verse of scripture that is quoted on countless occasions and finds its way onto plaques and coffee mugs.

> *"For I know the plans I have for you," declares the Lord, "plans to prosper you and not to harm you, plans to give you hope and a future".* **Jeremiah 29:11 (NIV)**

That is a great verse and it's most certainly true, but it would serve us well to consider the context. The people of God had been led away into captivity to a major city called Babylon. The reason God allowed this to happen is because the nation had forsaken His laws, turned their backs on Him, worshipped idols, intermingled with pagan nations and a long list of practices that would eventually end in judgment. As they waited out the seventy years of captivity that was prophesied, God gave them instructions to **pray for the city**. Those directives came from the merciful heart of God. You see, even while they were living out their justified captivity, the Lord wanted them to experience His grace and prosperity. So back up to verse seven where the Lord says,

> *Also, seek the peace and prosperity of the city to which I have carried you into exile. Pray to the Lord for it, because if it prospers, you too will prosper.* **Jeremiah 29:7 (NIV)**

Now, hopefully you don't feel that you have been "carried into exile" to the city you live in. Many times, we wish we could just relocate and escape some of the hindrances and limitations of the city we live in. "The grass always looks greener." As I write this book, The Father's House currently has people coming to our six campus locations from over 50 different cities. I would guess that many of you have complained about your city a time or two and asked God to "deliver you." Let me encourage you to take another approach. Pray for your city, seek its prosperity, and ask God to change the atmosphere, the economy, the spiritual climate, and the very culture. Then put some feet to your prayers and find a way to serve your city with the tangible love of Christ!

AT THE JUDGMENT

There is a glorious and terrifying scene that plays out in **Matthew 25**. It is glorious for those who know Christ and have lived lives of generosity and outreach, and terrifying for those who thought they were in good standing with God yet had no evidence of that love. They had head knowledge but lacked heart change. A theology without a practice that demonstrates the tangible love of God equals dead religion. Remember, these are not the qualifying factors that give us entrance to heaven, but the undeniable evidence that we have lived lives that magnify Jesus.

All the nations will be gathered in His presence, and He will separate the people as a shepherd separates the sheep from the goats. He will place the sheep at His right hand and the goats at His left. Then the King will say to those on His right, 'Come, you who are blessed by My Father, inherit the Kingdom prepared for you from the creation of the world. For I was hungry, and you fed Me. I was thirsty, and you gave Me a drink. I was a stranger, and you invited Me into your home. I was naked, and you gave Me clothing. I was sick, and you cared for Me. I was in prison, and you visited Me.'
Matthew 25:32-36 (NLT)

We will be a church that continues to love and finds new ways to serve the people in our city. We will honor and pray for our city leaders, be involved in community events, feed the hungry, bless the hurting, and invest our time and resources to make a difference. **Hopefully, we will show the tangible love of Jesus in such a way that it becomes undeniable to those who need Him.**

If God has brought you to one of our Father's House Church plants or campuses or you are a part of The Prison Church Network, I would encourage you to find a place to serve! Invest your most precious commodity, your time, to serve the "least of these" and help us reveal Jesus to a hurting world.

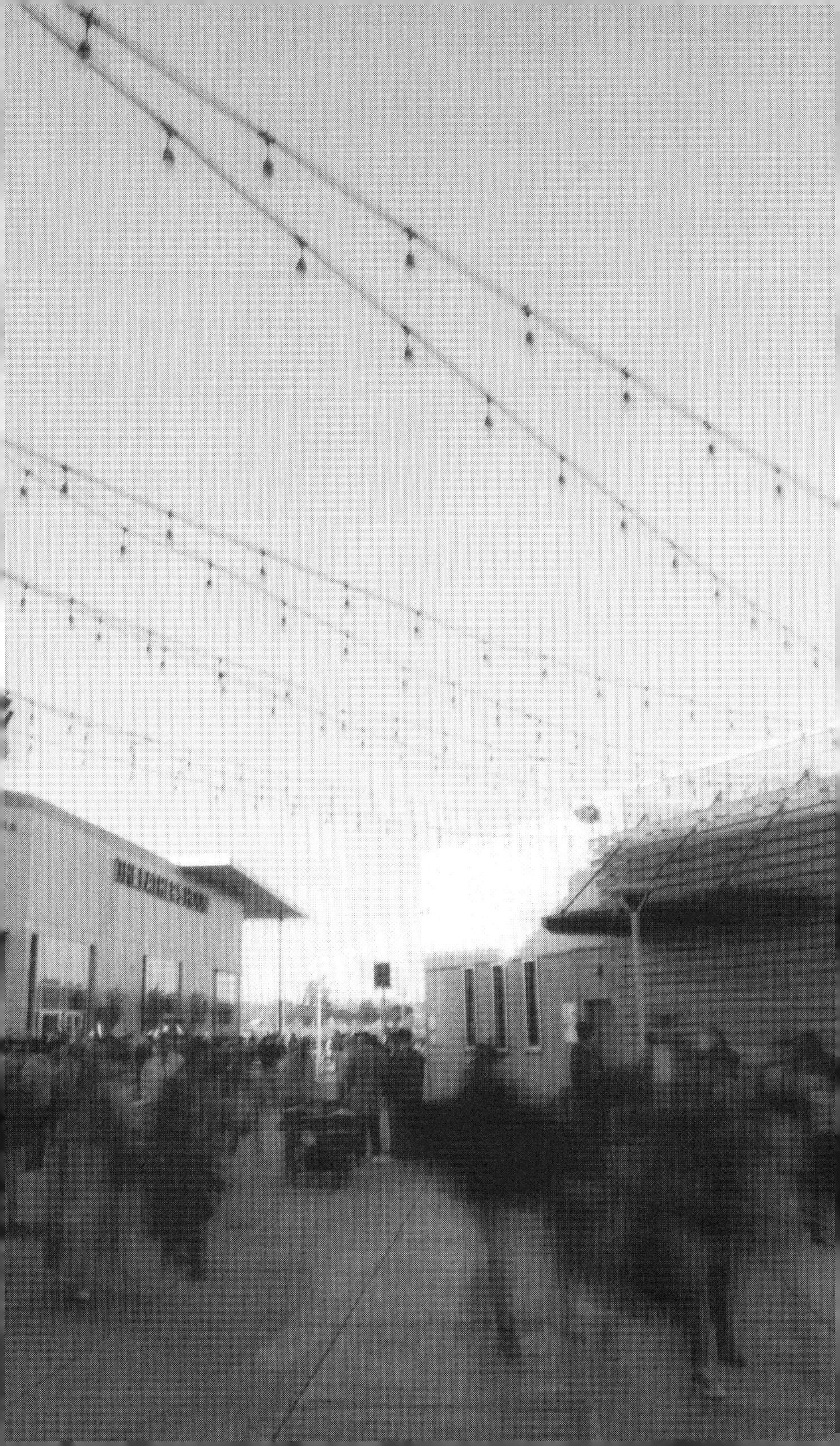

Chapter Ten

GO!

"We will live for the bigger picture, taking action locally and globally."

When Jesus was getting ready to leave our planet, He first gathered His disciples and gave them some final instructions. We know this passage of scripture as The Great Commission. Jesus came and told His disciples,

> *"I have been given all authority in heaven and on earth. Therefore, go and make disciples of all the nations, baptizing them in the name of the Father and the Son and the Holy Spirit. Teach these new disciples to obey all the commands I have given you. And be sure of this: I am with you always, even to the end of the age."*
> **Matthew 28:18-20 (NIV)**

Ironically and accurately stated, the first two letters of the word Gospel spell GO. This is the nature of what the church is all about. We are not called to survive, maintain, hunker down and make comfortable places of worship so that Christians can be a part of a local club. The Gospel is all about being empowered to fulfill the Great Commission, which requires getting up and going to places we have not been. **The trap for every church is to get to a place where we are content to maintain the good programs we have developed**, keeping the givers happy and repeating the cycles on a yearly basis. At The Father's House we have determined that we will continue to push each other toward the fulfillment of the Great Commission by not living satisfied with a local influence or a static place where we merely exist as a church. We are here to be empowered, discipled and then to GO.

In the first chapter of Acts we are given another charge from

Jesus and some clear instruction on how to strategize our mission.

> *"But you will receive power when the Holy Spirit comes on you; and you will be My witnesses in Jerusalem, and in all Judea and Samaria, and to the ends of the earth." After He said this, He was taken up before their very eyes, and a cloud hid Him from their sight.*
> **Acts 1:8-9 (NIV)**

The first thing Jesus told His disciples was that they would receive power to accomplish His mission. He told them to go, but to first wait. Get busy, but first become empowered. This empowerment is the arrival of the Holy Spirit that comes to baptize us and enable us to take not just the information about Jesus, but the power of God needed to confirm His message to the ends of the earth. This is why we wait on God, pray and ask for His divine enablement for every outreach and new venture. **The purpose for the power is to accomplish the mission of reaching the world**. Let's not get caught in the charismatic trap of just wanting more power, more encounters with God and deeper worship just because we enjoy being empowered. His power is for the purpose of going, reaching, and making disciples of all nations! If I'm lacking obvious power and motivation in my Christian journey, I need to ask myself if I'm on mission and going somewhere that requires fresh power, or am I just looking for a spiritual shot to keep me going?

As we perpetually live 'on mission', we can expect continual and increased empowerment.

OUR FOUR SPHERES OF INFLUENCE

1. Jerusalem
Jesus told His disciples that they would receive power and then they would go to "**Jerusalem**." This represents our home turf, our starting place of most obvious influence and responsibility. The disciples that waited for the power were right in the middle of downtown Jerusalem, which was the hub of the New Testament Church. Your "Jerusalem" is your family, friends, employees, co-workers, and all those who have been placed in your life. We believe God has called us to pray for, love, influence and invite to church all those who are in our Jerusalem.
If our gospel message and level of power does not work in our Jerusalem, then we should not worry about exporting it.

2. Judea
"Judea" represents our **regional influence**. As our church grows in power, influence, and gifting, we become increasingly responsible to minister to our region. This means that we move beyond our immediate sphere of influence (our family, friends, co-workers) and begin to see our cities and counties as our

field of ministry. This has a very practical application as we take action and go. The Gospel is best preached and understood when people's practical needs are being met. That's why Jesus fed the multitudes, healed the sick and made water into wine. He first touched the physical and then the spiritual.

In every city we launch a campus or plant a Father's House Church, we also make an immediate plan and investment to reach the practical needs of the city we are in. Right now (2024), our "Judea" has grown from our base camp in Vacaville to:

Napa Campus
East Bay Campus
Roseville Campus
Roseville Slavic and Ukrainian Campus
Calgary Canada Campus
13 Live Campuses in our State Prisons (and counting)
TFH San Francisco
TFH Oakland
TFH Orange County
TFH Natomas
TFH Elk Grove

As I write this chapter, we have new campuses and church plant plans that are on the drawing table, because we are determined that we will never slow down, back off or get comfortable with our current level of impact and expansion.

3. Samaria

"**Samaria**" represents the **crossing of cultural and ethnic boundaries**. If they could avoid it, the Jews did not even travel through Samaria. There was a cultural divide, where racism and prejudice were very strong and deeply entrenched in their history. When Jesus said, "*You will be My witnesses in... Samaria,*" He was telling them that they would deliberately cross those boundaries for the advancement of the Gospel. Our application today would be the intentional ministry that takes us out of our comfort zone and stretches us to reach people we would not run into at home in "Jerusalem" or "Judea." Let me encourage you to look for and get involved in ministry endeavors that take you to your "Samaria," where you are crossing cultural barriers, economic classes, getting outside your comfort zone and into the faith zone.

4. The Ends of the Earth

Since our church first began, it has been our delight to partner with international ministries, support numerous missionaries, and to be involved in many different nations. Through Global Reach we have had the privilege to purchase land, fund church building projects, construct community centers, build Bible colleges, support orphanages, dig wells, distribute medical supplies, host worship conferences and establish worship schools in many nations. What an awesome privilege when you realize God is using you to extend His Kingdom to the ends of the earth! Here are some of the nations that teams from The Father's House have traveled to and have a current investment in;

- Israel
- Philippines
- Brazil
- Turkey

- Uganda
- South Africa
- Haiti
- Guatemala

- India
- Austria
- Romania
- Turkey

- Mexico
- Nicaragua
- Sri Lanka
- Fiji

- Cambodia
- China
- Dominican Republic
- Nepal

- Poland
- Zimbabwe
- Ethiopia
- Kenya
- Togo

If you have never been involved in a mission's endeavor or endured that long plane ride to a distant land in order to preach the gospel and demonstrate the tangible love of God, I would strongly encourage you to do it! There is something about fulfilling this portion of the Great Commission that no other experience can touch. As a church we will continue to financially support, as well as send, people to the nations where God gives us relationships, opens doors of ministry and influence.

NO EXCUSES

Some have made the excuse that "We are supposed to reach our Jerusalem first and until we do that we should not worry about the rest." Yes, there are some translations of the Bible that say "Jerusalem first" but those do not give the most accurate translation of that verse. The more accurate word-for-word translations of the Bible, such as the English Standard Version (ESV), translate Acts 1:8 as "You will be My witnesses in Jerusalem and in all Judea and Samaria, and to the end of the earth." This is an important point to consider. It's never one or the other, or one before the other; it's always both Jerusalem and Samaria. Jesus was telling His first-century disciples, and all of us, that **when we are empowered with the Holy Spirit, we are to think and act both locally and globally at the same time.** Regardless of the size of our church or the level of our resources, the command is clear. Remember, Jesus gave this command to a small group of persecuted believers that had no organization, backing, funding, media, or a master plan to accomplish the task.

KINGDOM PERSPECTIVE

Years ago a man left our church because he did not approve of how we spent so much money on missions and asked people to raise their own support to go with us. His thought was, *"Why would you have people spend thousands of dollars to go when we could just send money and let the nationals do the ministry?"* The answer was simple. **Jesus said go. Money is temporal,**

not eternal. I also explained that the only way our church would have a heart for the nations is to go to the nations, stand on their soil, see the need with our own eyes and be moved with compassion. Jesus said "go" not "send a check."

Kingdom mindset causes us to live with a readiness to invest in people we may never see and travel to nations we may never visit again, yet we know that we are investing in the nonperishable, the eternal kingdom of God!

Our involvement in global missions and sending teams to the nations is an expensive endeavor, as well as time consuming and exhausting. There is no way we could sustain our involvement in missions without gaining and maintaining a Kingdom perspective. This means that we understand that **it's all about eternity and the Kingdom of God**. We are investing in things that will never be destroyed and a Kingdom that knows no end.

YOU CAN BE INVOLVED

As we update this book in 2024, The Lord has been speaking to our lead team about increasing our Global Reach in a way that will make a significant difference for eternity and a stronger partnership with the ministries we work with. It's quite simple and here's how it will work:

> **1. Start out by living as a tither;** that is, bringing the first and best to the Lord as we understand and practice that "The tithe belongs to the Lord" and we are returning to Him what He has entrusted to us.
>
> **2. Go beyond the tithe;** Ask the Holy Spirit to speak to you regarding what He would have you invest, monthly, to all that we are doing in the nations.
>
> **3. Give on the app or website:** simply go to the giving page at tfh.org and hit "Global Reach". You can also set up re-occurring giving and adjust that amount or discontinue at any time.

Remember: LIFE IS SHORT – ETERNITY IS REAL – PEOPLE MATTER MOST

What do you say we make a difference in the eternal destinations of as many people as possible in as many nations as God will empower us to reach? Let's live for the bigger picture, let's live with an awareness of the brevity of life and invest in the eternal!

> *"We must quickly carry out the tasks assigned us by the one who sent us. The night is coming, and then no one can work"*
> **John 9:4 (NLT)**

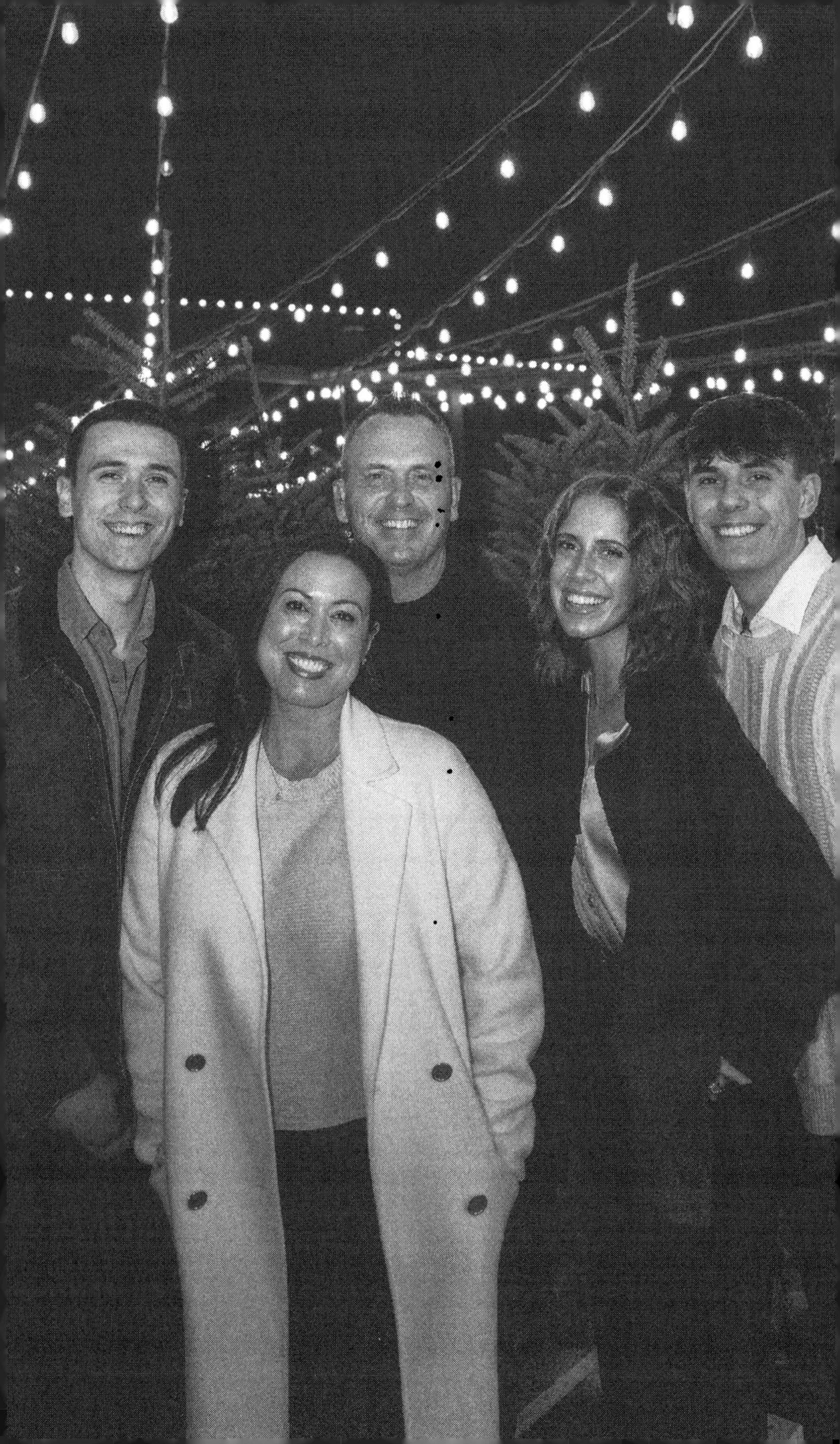

Chapter Eleven

ENJOY THE JOURNEY

"We will enjoy the journey; laugh hard, loud and often."

I love the fact that this value made our top-ten list. You might think laughing and having a good time would not have made the cut when you consider the serious nature of rescuing people from an eternity without God. Yet, the value of enjoying life, being filled with joy and laughter, is a high priority in the Scriptures and was modeled by the very life and attitude of Jesus. **Hebrews 1:9** is a statement made regarding Jesus and his countenance.

> *You love justice and hate evil. Therefore, O God (Jesus), your God (the Father) has anointed You, pouring out the oil of joy on You more than on anyone else.* **Hebrews 1:9 (NLT)**

This verse is letting us know that Jesus was the happiest guy in the room almost all of the time. The Greek word used for joy in this verse is *Agalliasis* = to jump for joy, to be happy, to rejoice exceedingly; be highly elated or jubilant. Commentaries agree that this verse is revealing that Jesus was a carrier of joy and that His joy level was obvious!

Many of us need to craft a new mental image of what Jesus looked like during His ministry on earth. If you're like me, you grew up with pictures of Jesus hanging in your home or your church. Most of these pictures were of a somber Jesus with long light-brown hair, blue-green eyes and a flawless complexion. Historically and biblically none of these attributes would be accurate. Jewish men of Jesus' day kept their hair cut and their beards trimmed. He probably had short hair, a dark complexion and he definitely did not have blonde tinted hair and blue-green eyes.

Another incorrect mental image is to picture Jesus as somber and contemplative. Yes, He wept, was moved with compassion, and became angry at times. Yet, His life would be best characterized as a life of joy, enjoying people, rejoicing, smiling, preferring the company of kids over adults, and probably laughing out loud at the parties. Jesus told us quite clearly that if we would stay connected to Him and abide in His love that we would experience the same effects of joy!

> *I have told you these things, that My joy and delight may be in you, and that your joy and gladness may be of full measure and complete and overflowing.* **John 15:11 (AMP)**

> *The thief comes only in order to steal and kill and destroy. I came that they may have and enjoy life, and have it in abundance –to the full, until it overflows.* **John 10:10 (AMP)**

There it is! Jesus not only came to destroy the works of the enemy but to ensure that we would enjoy our journey and live life to the fullest. This means that we will actually live our lives as Jesus did, with purpose and calling, on mission, leading others, serving the poor and broken, focused on eternity and overflowing with His joy.

JOY AND HAPPINESS

Let me clarify the difference between joy and happiness. Joy is a fruit of the spirit, an abiding spiritual condition regardless of circumstances. We can experience the Joy of the Lord no matter what life throws at us and we can actually express that joy, even if we are not feeling it.

> *Yet I will rejoice in the Lord!*
> *I will be joyful in the God of my salvation.*
> **Habakkuk 3:18 (NLT)**

In the previous verse, the prophet Habakkuk describes a fairly bleak situation that would not make anyone happy, yet we see the clear instruction to rejoice and be joyful as a matter of will. This would be one of those heart conditions and emotional states where we "act our way into feelings, instead of feel our way into actions."

Happiness is an emotional response to an environment or set of circumstances. We are called to live with both joy and happiness. We are to "be filled with the spirit" which includes all the attributes mentioned in Galatians 5:22, and we also want to live lives characterized by happiness. "Happy" and "blessed" are two words that are often interchangeable in scripture and are based on God's favor and interactions with us.

> *Happy is he who has the God of Jacob for his help, Whose hope is in the Lord his God.* **Psalm 146:5 (NKJV)**

Life is filled with trials, tragedies and seasons that do not provide happiness. There is a time to laugh and a time to weep and mourn, but they should be the minority of our lives, not the overarching attitude and emotion we experience.

> *Weeping may last through the night, but joy comes with the morning.* **Psalm 30:5 (NLT)**

> *Teach us to realize the brevity of life, so that we may grow in wisdom.* **Psalm 90:12 (NLT)**

Life is Short so Laugh Now! Allow me to paraphrase this concept. "Life is too brief to live it miserably." Let's laugh now, let's laugh hard and let's laugh often! One of the values and consistent behaviors of our leadership team is the fact that **we take our mission seriously and ourselves, not so much**. We have fun at every staff meeting, leadership meeting and creative meeting. Sometimes we push the envelope and have to reel it in a bit, but I'd much rather err on the fun side.

Years ago, I was visiting a church in Texas, and I was with a friend who was on staff. As we were catching up and enjoying one another's company I started cracking up over something he said. He replied with, "Ssshhhh, no laughing in the halls," to which I responded, "What? You're kidding!" He went on to quote one of their staff policies which stated that *this is a business environment so no laughing in the halls*. WOW! I remember thinking to myself that if I ever pastor a church or build a team, I will require laughing in the halls!

When Jesus conducted His ministry, the children loved to come to Him, sit on His lap and be near Him. Once, when the disciples tried to keep the children away from Jesus, He didn't take it calmly and let them know that the Kingdom is made up of those who have child-like faith, hearts, and demeanors. In the book, Possessing Joy: A Secret to Strength and Longevity, the author S. Backlund describes how psychologists have studied the laughing patterns of both children and adults. In this study they found that little kids laugh an average of 400 times a day while adults only laugh around 15-25 times per day. While life and responsibility can be blamed for much of the seriousness we exemplify as adults, we should make it a goal and continually pray to be "childlike" in this regard.

HUMOR IN CHURCH

You probably don't have a problem with having fun and laughing in church, but I want you to be aware that not everyone shares our value of having a good time in God's house. There are churches, pastors and authors that demand that humor is not fitting for the house of God and that "preaching is serious business so the pulpit is no place for humor." I could not agree less! I see laughter throughout the scriptures and there's not much argument that our sense of humor and ability to laugh and make others laugh is a gift from God. So why wouldn't we use it at church? Obviously, there are many forms of humor, topics and jokes that have no place in church or in the life of a believer, **but I can't think of a more appropriate setting to put a smile on people's faces where they can have a good laugh than in the House of God!**

> *A merry heart does good, like medicine, But a broken spirit dries the bones.* **Proverbs 17:22 (NKJV)**

Humor and laughter are like medicine to the burdened soul. What better place to take your medicine than when the Body of Christ comes together to worship, pray, and encourage one another!

TAKING INVENTORY

How often do you smile? How often do you laugh out loud? There are a variety of personalities and ways that people express joy and happiness. I am not suggesting that we should go outside of our personality types when responding with humor or laughter, but I do believe we should all convey as much joy and happiness as often as we can. For example, do you have people that you frequently plan time with that make you laugh? Do you avoid critical and depressing people that bring you down to their level? Do you "rejoice in your salvation," deliberately smile and experience joy by meditating on your salvation found in Jesus Christ? **Are you enjoying the journey?**

Let's consider that last question. Take a moment, even set down the book after you read this portion, and reflect on this line of questions. **Am I enjoying the journey of my life?** Do I anticipate tomorrow? Am I consistently involved in those things that bring me joy and am I eliminating the negative experiences? If not, why not? **Selah!** *Selah* is a Hebrew term that you will find frequently in the book of Psalms, and it means to pause, consider, think about what has been said, and reflect with the accompaniment of a musical instrument.

LET ME REPEAT MYSELF

Rejoice in the Lord always. I will say it again: Rejoice!
Philippians 4:4 (NIV)

When Paul is addressing all the churches, in his letter to the church of Philippi he commands them to "rejoice!" The word Paul is using simply means to be happy and to live with joy. This technique of repeating the same phrase was a common way to highlight an important point. Often Jesus would say "*again I tell you*" before He would emphasize a significant message. Therefore, when Paul is instructing the Church on how to live life he is simply saying, **"Be happy, have fun, live with joy! Oh and if I didn't make myself clear, let me tell you again, REJOICE!"**

So, if you have a moment, why not Selah on this point? Take a note pad, put on instrumental music and take some time to write down those things that bring you joy and those things that are stealing your joy. In light of what the scriptures say, consider your life and evaluate what adjustments and necessary changes you need to make now, in order to enjoy the journey and live life to the fullest.

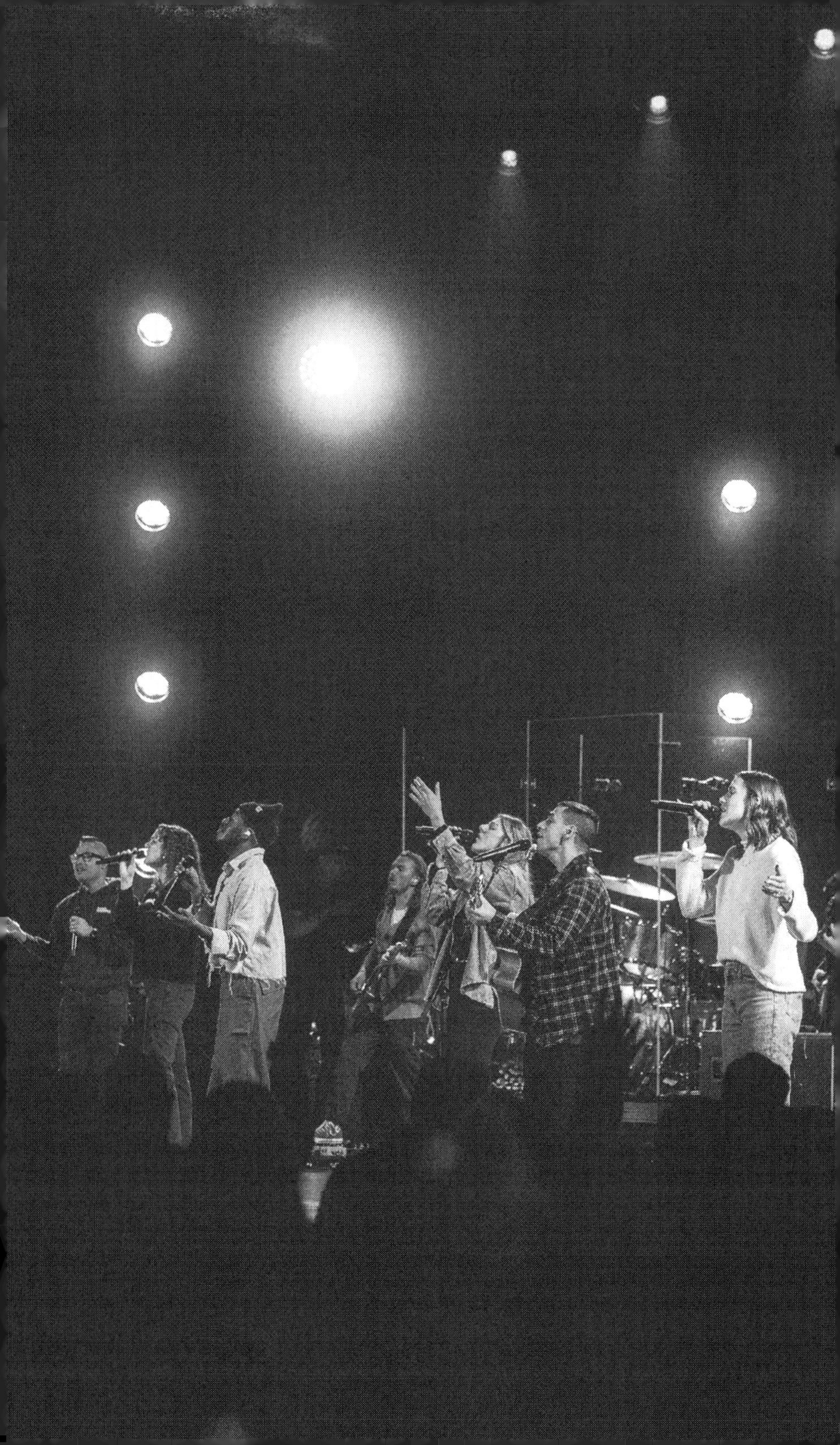

Chapter Twelve

SUPPORTING THE HOUSE

It's hard to ignore the topic of giving in the Bible. It is everywhere. From the Old to New Testaments, from the table of contents to the maps, you can't read even a couple chapters in any book without running into the topics of offerings, sacrifices, financial wisdom, tithing and generosity. Rarely would anyone who calls him or herself a follower of Christ oppose the idea of the Christian life being one of serving and giving. Where the varied opinions and doctrinal discussions come into view is when we start clarifying the teachings of Jesus, examining the practices of the New Testament Church and bringing application to our everyday lives. This is when we "put our money where our faith is." There will always be conflict and push-back when it comes to the issues of giving, simply because nothing else tests and reveals the motivation of the heart quite as clearly, quickly, and consistently as the Biblical instructions connected to our money.

> *Don't store up treasures here on earth, where moths eat them and rust destroys them, and where thieves break in and steal. Store your treasures in heaven, where moths and rust cannot destroy, and thieves do not break in and steal. Wherever your treasure is, there the desires of your heart will also be.*
> **Matthew 6:19-21 (NLT)**

Jesus is saying that our heart and desires are connected to our money. This includes our passions, affections, and the center of who we are. Giving, or lack thereof, is the easiest way to see where our affections, passions and priorities really are. Our heart is revealed by what we invest in. Look again at this verse in Matthew and consider the placement of the words. Jesus doesn't say, "Where your heart is, your treasure will end up." He says that our heart will follow our treasure. This is an important fact about money and other resources. You see, we all have control of where our heart will end up. We have the ability to govern the direction of our passions by what we invest in. Think about how this plays out in your own life when you buy a new car, invest in a new stock, purchase the airline tickets for the dream vacation, or buy the engagement ring. Your heart is immediately connected to those investments on a whole new level.

It's as if Jesus is saying, *"Don't invest in things that are perishing and get your heart all tied up in stuff that doesn't really matter.* ***Invest in the eternal things and live with your heart connected to eternity."***

WHEN GOD HAS YOUR HEART

When we truly give our lives to Christ, commit to follow Him, and live according to His Word, something begins to shift in our hearts that directs our treasures. **We begin to have a heart for His house, and we want to invest our resources in order to establish the kingdom of God through the local church**.

This is a work of the Holy Spirit and clear evidence that we have experienced a heart change. When the Holy Spirit was poured out on the New Testament Church there was immediate evidence that could be seen through how they handled their money.

> *There was an intense sense of togetherness among all who believed; they shared all their material possessions in trust. They sold any possessions and goods that did not benefit the community and used the money to help everyone in need.*
> **Acts 2:44-45 (VOICE)**

> *All the believers were united in heart and mind. And they felt that what they owned was not their own, so they shared everything they had. The apostles testified powerfully to the resurrection of the Lord Jesus, and God's great blessing was upon them all. There were no needy people among them, because those who owned land or houses would sell them and bring the money to the apostles to give to those in need.*
> **Acts 4:32-35 (NLT)**

That's some pretty radical giving and could only be accomplished by a work of the Holy Spirit. You can imagine the uprising and fallout if a pastor today asked people to sell everything they had and give the money to their church. Some pastors have done this, and it didn't end well. Yet, this was the behavior of the early church as they were filled with the Holy Spirit and passionate about being Christ followers.

The issue of giving is never about God needing your money or even the Church needing your money. It does take a lot of money to sustain an effective ministry, so when God is building His Church, He will always gather an army of generous people who will give, support, and build with Him. If I forfeit my opportunity to be a channel of resources, then someone else will step up and seize the opportunity. The issue is really not about God getting my money but getting my heart.

BIBLICAL PATTERNS AND PRINCIPLES

The Biblical patterns for financial generosity fall into two major categories as it pertains to New Testament believers:

1. Bringing the tithe
2. Giving freewill offerings

The Biblical word "tithe" means "tenth." The Bible teaches that the first tenth of all we earn or "all our increase" belongs to the Lord. **The reason we use the phrase "bring the tithe" is because we understand that it already belongs to God, and**

we are simply bringing back or "returning" what is already His. The truth about our ability to create and sustain an income is that it all comes from God in the first place. Not only our talent, but our ability to get an education, to find a good job, advance in our careers, and make a living is a gift from God.

He gave us the talent, health, opportunity, I.Q., and everything else we have used to succeed. When He asks us to bring back the first tenth, we are consistently reminded of whom the blessing comes from and that all we have comes from His hand. In reality, we don't just give our tithe; we bring it back. We are simply stewards of what we have been entrusted. This is a very healthy and accurate way to view the tithe; it belongs to God. It is His to receive, not ours to keep. We bring the tithe because it's holy to the Lord. This is also the principle of the first and best being holy, set apart and belonging to the Lord.

> *Should people cheat God? Yet you have cheated me! But you ask, 'What do you mean? When did we ever cheat you?' You have cheated me of the tithes and offerings due to me.* **Malachi 3:8 (NLT)**

> *Honor the Lord by giving him the first part of all your income, and He will fill your barns with wheat and barley and overflow your wine vats with the finest wines.* **Proverbs 3:9 (TLB)**

> *One-tenth of the produce of the land, whether grain from the fields or fruit from the trees, belongs to the Lord and must be set apart to Him as holy.* **Leviticus 27:30 (NLT)**

And this memorial pillar I have set up will become a place for worshiping God, and I will present to God a tenth of everything He gives me. **Genesis 28:22 (NLT)**

Throughout the Bible you will see that the first and the best belong to God. This is in essence the embodiment of the tithing principle. We always bring the first and the best. The tithe is never the leftovers. The first and the best belong to God because He is worthy! This is the foundation of true worship and the opening line of the Ten Commandments.

I am the Lord your God...You must not have any other god but Me. **Exodus 20:3 (NIV)**

We find this principle of "first and best" throughout the Bible, in both the Old and New Testaments. The firstborn is holy unto the Lord. The first fruits and first of the crops are to be brought to Him as an offering, a tithe. The first day of the week was set aside by the early Church as the day of worship and giving. In **I Corinthians 16:2** we are told, "*On Sunday, the first day of the week, I want each of you to set aside an amount, as God has blessed you*" (VOICE).

Tithing must be the first and the best. One of the strongest rebukes that God gave His people had to do with them bringing the leftovers. Tithing must be the first or it's not the tithe. I've talked with people who have said, "If I have extra after I pay all my bills and cost of living, then I will give to God." The reality is that there rarely seems to be any left over. When we bring the tithe into God's house, there is a promise that He will bless the rest. The bottom line of tithing is faith, a dependence and trust that the Lord is able to take care of all my needs as I trust Him with the first and the best.

We believe, and practice, that He can do more with 90% than we can with 100% of our income. We trust that He will rebuke the devourer, open heaven, and provide more than we could ever produce without His assistance. Until we trust and believe what His Word says about giving and receiving, it will be difficult to sustain a lifestyle of generosity and stewardship.

> *"Bring all the tithes into the storehouse so there will be enough food in My Temple. If you do," says the Lord of Heaven's Armies, "I will open the windows of heaven for you. I will pour out a blessing so great you won't have enough room to take it in! Try it! Put Me to the test."* **Malachi 3:10 (NLT)**

There is no doubt that tithing is a test for all of us. The results of that test come every pay period and clearly demonstrate where we are putting our trust when it comes to our money. The beautiful thing about tithing is God says, "T*est Me! Put Me to the test with your giving.*" God never fails a test!

FREQUENTLY ASKED QUESTIONS ABOUT TITHING

1. Isn't tithing an Old Testament command for those "under the law" and not for today?

Bringing the first and the best or "the tithe" is a principle that can be found as early as Cain and Abel in the Book of Genesis. This was around 2,500 years before the Old Testament law was established.

The phrase "tithe" or "tenth" and the principle of tithing predates the law by 430 years. Hundreds of years before God ever established covenant laws for His people, He set in motion the principle of bringing the first and best in the form of a tithe. This is a covenant based on faith and worship, not rules, guilt, or condemnation. Melchizedek blessed Abram with this blessing:

> *Blessed be Abram by God Most High, Creator of heaven and earth. And blessed be God Most High, who has defeated your enemies for you.* **Genesis 14:19-20 (NLT)**

Then Abram gave Melchizedek a tenth of all the goods he had recovered. Melchizedek is an Old Testament Christophany, which is a pre-incarnate appearance of the Son of God. So basically, **Jesus shows up to bless the "father of all who would believe" and Melchizedek's response of worship and faith was to tithe (see Hebrews 7:1-10)**.

Jacob made a covenant to tithe hundreds of years before the law was given. This was simply a faith and worship response to the faithfulness of God and a further establishing of the tithing principle. He declares in **Genesis 28:22**, "*And this memorial pillar I have set up will become a place for worshiping God, and I will present to God a tenth of everything He gives me*" (NLT).

When Jesus was dealing with the religious leaders who were focused on enforcing the law, He instructed them to continue to tithe but not to forget the most important elements of the law: mercy and justice. In fact, **there are no New Testament scriptures that would indicate a discontinuation of the practice of tithing; it is only confirmed.**

> *For you are careful to tithe even the tiniest income from your herb gardens, but you ignore the more important aspects of the law— justice, mercy, and faith. You should tithe, yes, but do not neglect the more important things.* **Matthew 23:23 (NLT)**

Galatians 3:29 tells us that "*if we belong to Christ then we are the true children of Abraham*" and that all the promises that God made to Abraham belong to us as we live out the covenant of faith. As children of Abraham, we are to live a lifestyle of tithing and bringing God the first and the best.

2. Shouldn't a New Testament believer give as the Spirit leads instead of a set percentage?

The New Testament never teaches that tithing ceases once we are under grace. Rather, giving offerings is encouraged above the tithe. Once the grace of God hit the New Testament Church, they gave everything. They claimed that "*none of their possessions were their own*" **(see Acts 2-4)**. The tithe was the starting block for New Testament givers in the Church. Yes, we should be led by the Spirit and give as the Holy Spirit moves us regarding offerings and sacrificial gifts where God is testing our faith. The understanding of the tithe is that it belongs to the Lord, and it is the starting place of giving for covenant people.

3. Do I have to tithe to the local church? What if I give to other people and ministries?

I've heard people say, "*Oh, I tithe by giving to a family member or a friend who is doing some missionary work, and I give to various organizations as I feel led.*" Even though you may be genuinely led to give to legitimate organizations, this is not the biblical instruction about tithing. In **Exodus 23:19** God tells His people to, "*bring only the best crops from your first harvest into the house of the Eternal God*" (VOICE).

The tithe is to be brought to the House or the storehouse, which in New Testament application is the Church, the place where you are connected to the Body, fed, and overseen by God-appointed leaders. Any giving above and beyond that is up to the individual and would fall into the category of offerings.

4. Should I tithe if I can't afford it?

Let's turn this question around. Can you afford not to tithe? Another way to look at it is that you will never know if God's promises of provision are true until you "*test Him in this*" **(Malachi 3)**. Ultimately, tithing is about trusting. If we cannot trust God with the first and best, then we are dealing with a faith issue, not a lack of money issue. The reality is we all have been entrusted with "seed" (money). Some have been entrusted with more than others, for sure, yet the principles of faith and multiplication apply to the wealthy, as well as the widow who has only one meal worth of flour and oil **(I Kings 17:10-16)**. I would encourage every believer to get familiar with the principles in these portions of scripture and put God to the test in your finances **(see Matthew 6:25-33, 2 Corinthians 9:6-11, Philippians 4:19, Malachi 3:10, Proverbs 3:9-10)**.

5. Am I robbing God if I don't tithe?

Let me just go ahead and walk on some thin ice here. At times pastors and preachers boldly preach that if you don't tithe you are robbing God, and thieves don't make it to heaven! I do not fully agree with that position for the following reasons. That's a big club and a pretty heavy message for new believers who are trying to wrap their minds around giving the first 10% of their income to the Lord. We need to be careful with **Malachi 3:8** regarding non-tithers being thieves. We are all on a journey of faith and maturity where God requires obedience at differing levels. He doesn't expect the infants (baby Christians) to walk or the toddlers (young in the Lord) to get a job and support the family.

I am not comfortable preaching that non-tithers are robbing God simply because God's expectations in this area are based on our faith level and maturity in Him. At the same time, the investment of our treasure or lack thereof, is a clear indication of where our heart is. If someone knows the scriptures, is an established Christian, has been convicted about tithing and giving, yet justifies why they do not give, they are revealing a heart that has been hardened to the Word of the Lord or a heart that does not truly belong to Christ. How can we say we know Him and have been changed by His love, indwelt by His power and not be givers? It's impossible! **James 4:17** reminds us that *"it is sin to know what you ought to do and then not do it"* (NIV). The bottom line is: **If He has your heart, He will have your finances.**

GIVING FREE-WILL OFFERINGS

The second area of New Testament giving is regarding free-will offerings. Simply put, this is anything that we give to God above the tithe. This would include special offerings for missionary work, benevolence, and special projects such as feeding the poor, giving our time, clothes, or other resources. Determine in your heart what you want to give based on how God has blessed you.

> *Remember this—a farmer who plants only a few seeds will get a small crop. But the one who plants generously will get a generous crop. You must each decide in your heart how much to give. And don't give reluctantly or in response to pressure. 'For God loves a person who gives cheerfully.' And God will generously provide all you need. Then you will always have everything you need and plenty left over to share with others.*
> **2 Corinthians 9:6-9 (NLT)**

This was not an exhortation about tithing, but a special offering that was being collected for impoverished believers in another nation. Give with a thankful heart and never out of pressure or manipulation. "*Don't give reluctantly or in response to pressure. For God loves a person who gives cheerfully.*" This is a very important point. God never wants us to give out of a motivation of fear, pressure, guilt, or in response to emotional hype. Our motives should always be with faith, thankfulness, and anticipation of what our seeds of faith will produce! Whenever there is an opportunity to give above and beyond, I would simply encourage you to pray about it with an open heart and respond to the leading of the Holy Spirit.

WE DETERMINE THE LEVEL OF BLESSING WE LIVE IN.

Are your finances blessed? Have you given God plenty of good reasons to entrust you with more? If God were to financially bless you, would you look forward to being a greater giver? What do you do with extra seed? Do you sow it back into the kingdom or do you consume it? Have you determined that you would give more in the future than you have in the past?

> *The same One who has put seed into the hands of the sower and brought bread to fill our stomachs will provide and multiply the resources you invest and produce an abundant harvest from your righteous actions. You will be enriched in*

every way so that you can be generous on every occasion.
2 Corinthians 9:10-11 (VOICE)

The reason God wants to give us more seed is so that we can be generous on every occasion! **Don't forget, it's God who gives the seed to the sower, not the eater!** When we consume all our seed and spend all we have on ourselves, then we are positioning ourselves to be fully responsible for our future income without God's involvement. The Bible tells us that when we sow what He has put in our hands and continue to increase our giving, He has already determined that He will entrust us with more!

What are the Results of a Local Church with Members that Tithe?

Let's take a few moments to consider what an army of generous, tithing, giving believers can do to advance the kingdom of God. At the writing of this book our church is being consistently supported by approximately 20-25% of the members. Although that's far above the national average of 4%, it's only 25% of our potential! I truly believe that God wants everyone who calls our church their home to have a heart for the house, tithe to the local church, give offerings above and beyond, experience God's blessing and together build an amazing church for the glory of God! Here are some of the results that come from
consistent giving:

- The Great Commission fulfilled as people far from God find life in Christ through the funded ministries of the local church.
- Families are brought back together, and marriages are rescued, restored and strengthened.
- Children are raised in the House to know and serve God for the rest of their lives!
- Missionaries are supported, and ministries are invested in, all over the world.
- The hungry and hurting in our city are consistently fed, served, clothed, and helped.
- Other churches, ministries and organizations are encouraged and helped to fulfill God's call for them.
- Young people are changed and trained through student ministries and internships. This is the next generation that will lead the Church.
- Prisoners are reached with the gospel
- The atmosphere and future of our city is being transformed through the presence of a strong and thriving local church.
- Heaven is populated and hell vacated through the investments of giving people.

A Personal Word:
My wife Donna and I have been tithing since we were married in 1982. Through hard times, lean years, unemployment, and seasons of confusion we made a determination to tithe no matter what. I can testify that I have never seen God fail to provide for us, and furthermore, He has continued to prosper us with financial increase. When we started The Father's

House, we determined that we would be a church that tithed to missions and other ministries and invest generously into our city. We have seen the supernatural provision and favor of God since we planted the church in 1997, and we are convinced that the best is yet to come. I would encourage you to be a giver and determine in your heart to be a life-long tither.

In **Matthew 6:20-21** we are encouraged to, "*store your treasures in heaven, where they will never become moth eaten or rusty and where they will be safe from thieves. Wherever your treasure is, there your heart and thoughts will also be*" (NIV). Will you invest the treasure God has given you? Settle that question. Make the commitment once and for all, and you will never regret it, not in this life and especially in the life to come when we stand before God to see what our giving accomplished for eternity.

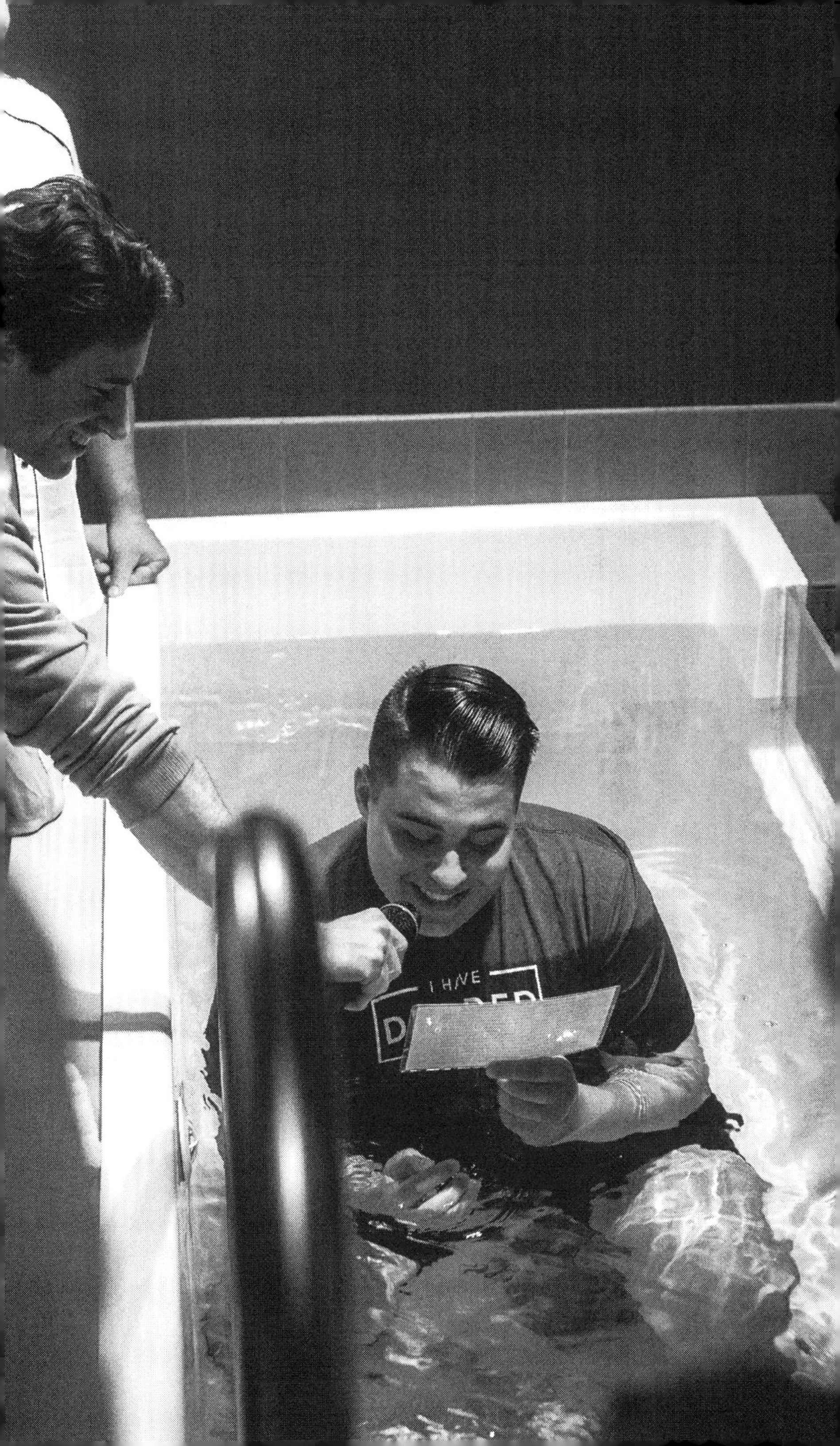
I HAVE

Chapter Thirteen

MEMBERSHIP: THE CHURCH I WANT TO JOIN

"And the Lord added to their number daily those who were being saved." Acts 2:47 (NLT)

The Church has been defined and redefined for centuries. It has been attacked, misunderstood, misrepresented, and poorly marketed to the consumers. The Church has been caricatured in a negative light in almost every movie that refers to it, yet the Church remains alive, growing and assembling more believers and seekers than at any other time in history! The primary reason for the success and resilience of the Church must go back to the power of the statement that was made by the Founder.

> *"And upon this rock I will build my Church, and all the powers of hell will not conquer it." –Jesus*
> **Matthew 16:18 (NLT)**

WHAT IS CHURCH AND WHY WOULD I JOIN?

If you say the word "church" to ten different people, there will be at least ten different images and emotions connected with the word. Some responses may include statements such as:

"Church is an irrelevant gathering of religious people."

"It is stained glass, rituals and a bunch of rules and regulations."

"It is a boring waste of a Sunday morning."

"They just want your money."

"My parents made me go when I was young."

One of the most common reasons people give for not attending church is because they believe it is full of hypocrites. They think that churchgoers are close-minded people who live one way on Sunday and another way the rest of the week. While I cannot argue that we do have our share of these types of people in attendance, it does not negate the beauty and eternal quality of the Church Jesus is building. If you were raised in church, you can probably recall the familiar sounds of a Sunday service, the musty smells of an old building, and a potluck at the park on a warm Sunday afternoon. Man, I loved those days. They are by far my sweetest memories of being raised in church. Unfortunately, not everyone has a positive image or opinion regarding church life and the Body of Christ.

THE CHURCH IS NOT MAN'S IDEA

Based on the hypocrisy that people see throughout Church history, you would think that it was man's idea. When looking at the abuse of power, the man-made religious trappings and empires built to honor men or denominations, you could easily buy into the false narratives and assumptions that the organization of Christ followers had to be conceived from the minds of men. But this is not true. The fact is that the Church is and has always been God's plan. The Church by definition is the assembly of those who have been "called out and called together"(I Peter 2:9 NIV).

The Church is the identifiable assembly of those who are following the teachings of Jesus because they have been drawn together by His Spirit and are being changed by His grace.

The Church includes sinners, saints, seekers, and cynics. It is a work in progress, a mystery and at times an oxymoron. The Church is a wonder and ultimately the object of Christ's affections. It is the most important gathering of all time and eternity! When Jesus returns it will be to claim His Bride, His Church, the desire of His heart for those that have been called out and called together. The Church is a big deal! It's a big deal to God and it's a big deal to us. **When we live with the revelation that the Church is God's design, God's prize, and God's eternal romance, it will cause us to see the true Church through His eyes and acquire a heart for the House!**

ASSEMBLY REQUIRED

I've grown to resent the words, "assembly required." You see, I have four grandkids to whom I have become (or so it seems) the primary toy assembler. And like some of you, I also dabble in the area of home improvement and can be found at Ikea, Home Depot, Costco, or online, purchasing the next great item that will make life complete and my wife happy. The problem with getting the do-it-yourself box version is in the assembly. As I stare at an instruction booklet the size of a small phone book and a pile of spare parts, I always come to the same conclusion: "It didn't look that complicated in the store." And so, with a tension of hope and trepidation I gather the required tools and dive in. The motivation behind the assembly is quite obvious. There is a box full of individual parts that won't function or do anyone any good until assembled properly.

So, it is with the body of Christ. It's not enough to say, "I'm a Christian and I've got things worked out between Jesus and myself." The biblical pattern is clear. Until we are connected with others and committed to building something bigger than all of us, we have not yet been assembled into the Church.

A Christian who lives in isolation is not a biblical believer. It is when we are vitally connected to the gifts and abilities of others that we begin to thrive in our relationship with God. So while the assembly process can seem tedious or unrewarding, it's God's design that enables us to live our lives to the fullest.

> *For no matter how significant you are,*
> *it is only because of what you are a part of.*
> **1 Corinthians 12:19 (MSG)**

Many people will say, "I'm a Christian, but I don't like going to church." An even stronger version is, "I know Jesus but I can't stand Church." These types of statements are an insult to Christ and a revealing of a deceived heart. The assembled Body of Christ is the masterpiece of God Himself. Random, lost, diverse people coming together in unity around the person of Jesus in the power of the Holy Spirit is a divine mystery. When God calls us out of darkness, He calls us to join with one another together under a spiritual covering as part of the Church. To be a member means that we get together and we stay together.

We are the Church, and we gather as the church. Consistent church attendance is a clear biblical mandate and not a pastor's master plan to keep the numbers up!

> *And let us consider how we may spur one another on toward*
> *love and good deeds,* ***not giving up meeting together,***
> ***as some are in the habit of doing,*** *but encouraging one*
> *another— and all the more as you see the Day approaching.*
> **Hebrews 10:24-25 (NIV)**

I've talked to too many Christians who have developed a real flimsy theology about the Church and their lack of need to connect or identify with a particular one. Perhaps they have just never received clear teaching about the importance and authority of the local church. They make comments such as, *"I don't need the Church to please God"* or *"I'm a part of the universal Church and do not need to commit to one in particular."* These remarks usually come from people who have either received some bunk teaching, been wounded by an unhealthy church in the past, or are unwilling to submit to spiritual authority.

They may also just want to claim the benefits of salvation without committing to serving and giving according to biblical standards. The sooner we realize that we need the Body of Christ and that our contribution is essential, the sooner we can get on with growing and living a life of significance. The Apostle Paul shares this concept of the Church being one Body in Christ when stating, *But God made our bodies with many parts, and He has put each part just where He wants it. What a strange thing a body would be if it had only one part! Yes, there are many parts, but only one body. The eye can never say to the hand, 'I don't need you.' The head can't say to the feet, 'I don't need you'.*
1 Corinthians 12:18-21 (NLT)

Membership and identification with a pastor or team of pastors is a clear way of saying, "I need you." Our desire is that you would be connected to the flow of life that is only found in and through the Body of Christ.

The Church is led by "God-Appointed Leaders"

> *Here are some of the parts* **God has appointed for the church:** *First are apostles, second are prophets, and third are teachers.... those who have the gift of leadership.* **1 Corinthians 12:28 (NLT)**

This is what differentiates the Church from a gathering of believers in a home group. Now don't jump to the wrong conclusion here. We love home groups and encourage people continually to be a part of one. The big idea is that God appoints pastors and leaders to equip, oversee, lead, preach, teach, and take responsibility for the Church in a particular geographic location. You can be a Christ follower and not attend a church (not sure why you would want to do that) and you can be a church without a building. You can meet in a field, under a tree, or in a mini-van and still be a church, but **you cannot be a church without God appointed New Testament leadership.**

> *Now these are the gifts Christ gave to the Church: the apostles, the prophets, the evangelists, and the pastors and teachers. Their responsibility is to equip God's people to do His work and build up the Church, the Body of Christ.* **Ephesians 4:11-12 (NLT)**

The valid questions every Christ follower should ask are:
- *Am I connected to a church that is structured according to the New Testament patterns and mandates?*
- *Am I under true spiritual covering, both accountable to and receiving from, God-appointed leaders?*
- *Am I bringing my part to the body, serving, and contributing*

according to the grace and gifts God has given me?
- Am I identified with a healthy, Jesus-centered, Bible-teaching church?

DO I HAVE TO BE A MEMBER?

Here is where it gets a bit subjective. As we have discussed, it is clear in scripture that you have been called into an assembly, The Lord "adds you to the church" to submit to and identify with spiritual leadership. In the New Testament we are exhorted to assemble with other believers consistently. But there is nothing in scripture that says you have to sign on
the dotted line. So, while we ask people to formally become a member by agreeing to the vision and values of the House, we fully understand that **this is not a technical requirement in scripture; neither does it get you any closer to God!** So why choose a formal membership? The simple answer is the biblical words, **"joined and added."**

> In Him the whole building is **joined** together and rises to become a holy temple in the Lord. **Ephesians 2:21 (NLT)**

> Those who accepted His message were baptized, and about three

*thousand were **added to their number** that day.* **Acts 2:41 (NLT)**

*...praising God and enjoying the favor of all the people. And the Lord **added to their number** daily those who were being saved.* **Acts 2:47 (NLT)**

*Nevertheless, more and more men and women believed in the Lord and were **added to** their number.* **Acts 5:14 (NLT)**

It becomes very clear in the previous verses that God joins or connects us together to become His body here on earth. Those who are being saved are being added to "their number," which reveals that **there was clearly an identifiable, quantifiable and recorded number of believers as the Church grew.** There was a list, a scroll, a document, a headcount, and a membership of sorts. Now, it's not worth splitting theological hairs over this one; let the smart guys do that. The point is clear that when someone was saved, they were added to a number and joined to a congregation or assembly of believers. I would in no way be dogmatic about having individuals sign a formal membership in order to be received into our church. But I would recommend that they identify with a local church, submit to the spiritual leadership of that house, and promote and protect the God-given vision and mission. They should serve with their time, talent, and resources in order to see the Church thrive and impact their city. **All that sounds like membership to me.** We have found that a simple membership agreement with a written commitment is the clearest and most effective way for people to recognize and determine where they are connecting and for what purpose. Do you have to become a member to attend a church? No, not at all, but if you are going to connect, receive spiritual covering, use your gifts and abilities, and walk in unity with the vision of the House, **membership is the key!**

HOW DO I JOIN?

Pray about it. Prayerfully determine if this is the place where God has led you and is planting you. If you will give this some time in prayer and waiting on God, He will be faithful to let you know. You will have a peace and a "green light" to make the commitment.

> *My sheep hear my voice, and I know them, and they follow Me.*
> **John 10:27 (ESV)**

Currently, membership is offered through our DISCOVER Class. This is where we cover what it means to become a member of the church, serve, join a group, and grow in the Word through Biblical Studies.

IN CONCLUSION

Here is a list of qualities, behaviors and attitudes mentioned in the previous chapters, to personally look for in a church before you become a member. Whether it is here at The Father's House, a different local church, or a church in another city, I would highly recommend that you bring these **ten questions** to the table and prayerfully consider the answers before you join.

1. Is it Christ centered?
Do they talk about Jesus, preach about Jesus, worship Jesus and keep Jesus at the center of the worship, Word and overall experience?

2. Are people being saved?
This seems like a basic question, yet the majority of churches in our nation rarely see someone make a decision to follow Christ during their gatherings. Are people coming to Christ, being born again, baptized in water and added to the body of Christ on a consistent basis?

3. Is the Bible taught and preached?
There are obviously different styles, techniques and methods of teaching the scriptures and there is room for all of them. The question is, do they teach from the Bible? Do they read the Bible, break down Scripture and keep the communication based in the truth of the Word? Theological and doctrinal accuracy is a must in regard to the non-negotiable

teachings of scripture (*i.e. the deity of Jesus, the inherency of the Word, the realities of an eternal heaven and hell*).

4. Are they involved with world missions?
Do they support missions, send teams and invest in other nations? Does it reflect in the budget and the passion of the leaders? Are missions on the front burner?

5. Are they generous?
We all know that churches biblically receive offerings and encourage people to give. Does the leadership of the church model the behavior it's encouraging in the members and does the budget or yearly financial statement testify to their generosity?

6. Is there good financial accountability?
Do they have outside audits, healthy business practices, checks and balances within the organization? Does the pastor personally control the checkbook (never a good thing) and is there an annual budget report? Are they in good standing with local businesses and current on their bills? These are highly spiritual and important issues for a church.

7. Are they serving their community?
That is, are they getting outside the four walls of the church and being the tangible love of Christ to their city? Are they serving the poor and loving the broken in an obvious and consistent way?

8. Are the gifts and power of the Holy Spirit a priority?

I know this gets subjective depending on people's theology and experience, yet it is far too important to go unspoken due to semantics. Another way to ask would be, "Is the obvious presence and power of God moving during the services?"

9. Do they have big vision?

You can have big vision in a small town! I can testify. You can have big vision when there are only 10 people in the room. You can have big vision with no money. The question to ask is whether or not the church is living with a God-sized vision of a preferable future for their community that inspires you and requires big faith?

10. Are they enjoying the Journey?

Is there a tangible joy in the staff and during the gatherings? Do people on stage have a sense of humor and are the leaders not taking themselves too seriously? Can you laugh while in a church service? This is important to our team and grounded in scripture. *(refer to Chapter 11)*

There are also other valid questions that could extend the list such as:

- Do they have a heart for, and a focus on, Israel?
- Do they invest in marriages and family ministries?
- Are youth and student ministries a priority?
- Are they welcoming to anyone who walks in the door?
- Do they have consistent prayer meetings?

- Are they reaching out to, and working with, other churches in their city and region?

You may have other questions, so ask away, pray hard and make a commitment to join a healthy, growing local church. Obviously, if the church is new and just putting all of this together it will be a work in progress and the questions will be answered at a variety of levels. The questions listed above refer to established churches that have been around for a minimum of five years or more. By God's grace we are attempting to develop the kind of church that identifies and builds upon these values. We have a long way to go, but I do believe we can say a solid "yes" to these membership questions.

THE HEART FOR HIS HOUSE

In light of God's design for the Body of Christ, the New Testament pattern of being added and joined, there are clear benefits of being vitally connected to a healthy church. If you are floating between churches or have never prioritized membership in a local church, I would encourage you to reconsider. If God is leading you to The Father's House and you are prayerfully considering becoming a member, I would encourage you to make the move. His House is a safe haven for broken, messed up, non-religious people who are far from God! It is our vision, mission, and "Heart for the House" to be a place where those far from God can come and know that they are among a group of people who are all being forgiven, healed, and restored. We are all in process. The Body of Christ will be stronger, and your life will be blessed when you are connected and committed to a local church. Remember, even with all its flaws and struggles, **"Christ loved the Church and gave Himself up for her" (Ephesians 5:25 NIV).**

If the content of this book resonates with your spirit and you are ready to fully commit to the Church Jesus is building, I want to personally invite you to go all in and get planted in this House. As we anticipate the soon and eminent return of the Lord, I want you to be able to stand before Him knowing you have invested your life into what He gave His very life for..... THE CHURCH!